Learn Text Analytics and NLP using R

Step by step labs for beginners

Data Analytics Curriculum, LLC

About the Publisher

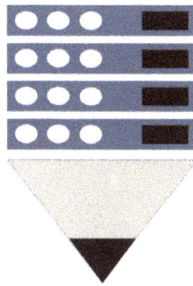

Data Analytics Curriculum

Data Analytics Curriculum, LLC creates approachable, visually engaging educational materials that make data science and technology accessible for learners from high school to college and independent study.

Please see our website or TPT online store for additional titles and resources such as slides, additional book forms, content (non lab) textbooks to accompany these labs, solution guides and other resources to help you teach and learn.

Additional resources available:

Website: https://www.dataanalyticscurriculum.com

Contents

Contents

Lab 1

Intro to R and RStudio

What is R and Why Use It?

R is a powerful and free programming language created specifically for statistical computing and data analysis. It has become popular across various fields such as data analytics, machine learning, and statistical analysis due to its extensive range of specialized packages tailored for data manipulation and interpretation. One of R's key strengths lies in its excellent data visualization capabilities, which allow users to create clear and insightful graphics. Additionally, it boasts strong libraries that support both statistical methods and machine learning techniques, making it a versatile tool for data professionals.

The language also benefits from a large and active community that contributes to its continuous improvement and offers support to users. Complementing R is RStudio, an Integrated Development Environment (IDE) that enhances the user experience by providing a more accessible interface, features like syntax highlighting, and various tools that help streamline the management of data projects, making it easier for both beginners and experienced users to work efficiently with R.

Part 1: Installing R and RStudio

Step 1: Download and Install R

Visit the R Project website: Go to https://www.r-project.org/

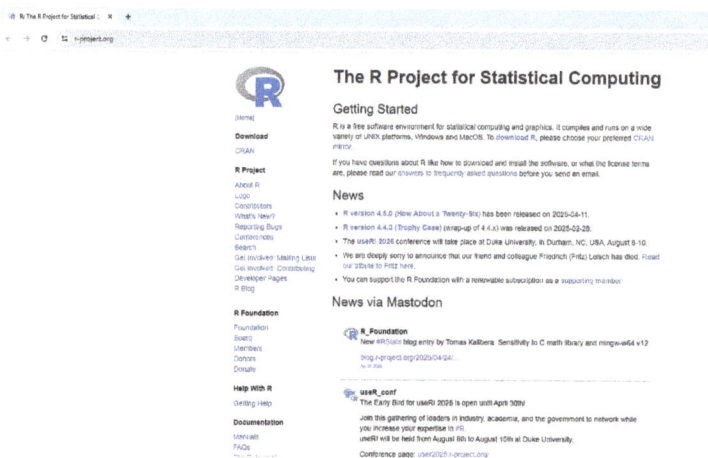

To install R, start by clicking on "CRAN" (Comprehensive R Archive Network) in the left sidebar of the website. Next, choose a mirror location that is close to you—any mirror in the USA works well for users in the United States. Then, select your operating system. For Windows, click on "Download R for Windows," then "base," and finally "Download R 4.x.x for Windows." Mac users should click on "Download R for macOS" and download the appropriate .pkg file for their system. If you are using Linux, follow the specific instructions provided for your distribution. Once the download is complete, run the installer and proceed with the default settings by clicking "Next" through the installation prompts.

Step 2: Download and Install RStudio

Note: You must install R first before installing RStudio, as RStudio requires R to function.

Visit RStudio's website: Go to https://posit.co/downloads/

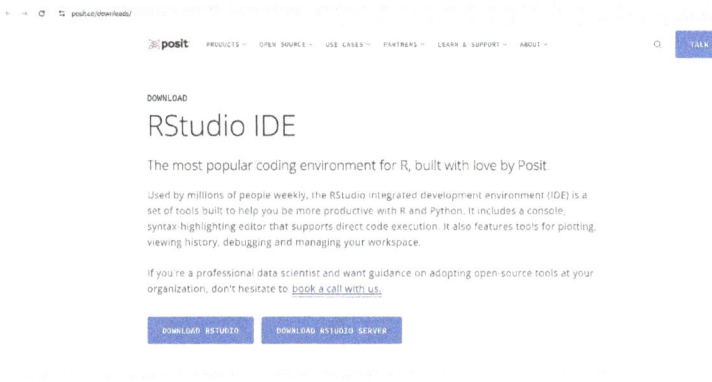

To install RStudio, scroll down the webpage until you find the section for RStudio Desktop, which is the free version. Click on "Download RStudio Desktop," then choose and download the installer that matches your operating system. Once the download is complete, run the installer and proceed with the default settings by simply clicking "Next" through the setup process.

Step 3: Verify Installation

Open RStudio (not R directly - we'll always use RStudio)

You should see a window with four panes (or three if it's your first time). In the bottom-left pane (Console), you should see something like:

If you see this, congratulations! You're ready to start using R.

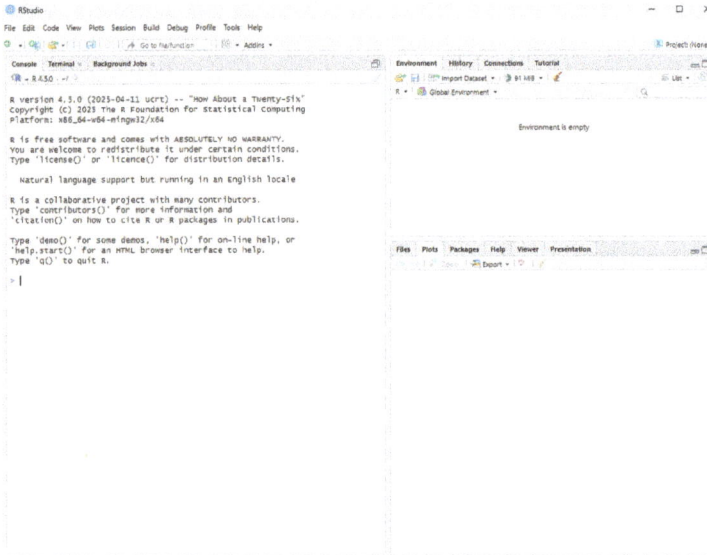

Part 2: The RStudio Interface

When you open RStudio, you'll see several panes. Initially there are three however go under file and do new R Script and the Script Editor appears.

Script Editor (Top-Left)

The Script Editor, located in the top-left panel of RStudio, is where you write and save your R scripts. It functions like a text editor specifically designed for writing R code, allowing you to organize and save your work for future use. From this panel, you can easily run individual lines or entire sections of code directly to the Console, making it a convenient space for developing and testing your code as you work through data analysis tasks.

Console (Bottom-Left)

The Console, found in the bottom-left panel of RStudio, is where R commands are executed. You can type commands directly into this space and see the results appear immediately below, making it useful for quick tests or interactive work. It's also where any code you run from the Script Editor will be processed, allowing you to view outputs, error messages, and other feedback in real time.

Environment/History (Top-Right)

The Environment/History panel, located in the top-right corner of RStudio, provides useful information about your current R session. The Environment tab displays all the data objects you've created, such as datasets, variables, and functions, allowing you to keep track of what's available in your workspace. The History tab keeps a record of all the commands you've run, making it easy to review, reuse, or modify previous code without having to retype it from memory.

Files/Plots/Packages/Help (Bottom-Right)

The Files/Plots/Packages/Help panel, located in the bottom-right corner of RStudio, serves several important functions. The Files tab lets you browse the files and folders on your computer, making it easy to locate and open your work. The Plots tab displays any graphs or visualizations you generate in R, allowing you to review and navigate through them. The Packages tab is where you can manage your R packages—these are add-on tools that extend R's capabilities, and you can install, load, or update them from this tab. Finally, the Help tab provides access to R's built-in documentation, offering detailed explanations and usage examples for functions and packages whenever you need guidance.

Part 3: Basic R Concepts

As a data analytics student, you'll primarily be running existing scripts rather than writing code from scratch. THIS IS NOT A PROGRAMMING COURSE OR BOOK. It is nice to have a programming background however the focus here is on USING and modifying existing scripts to perform data analytics tasks. You should be able to do this with a minimal programming background and should need to do little programming from scratch.

Working with Scripts

To open an existing R script in RStudio, go to the File menu, click on "Open File," and then select your .R file from your computer. Once your script is open, you can run your code in several ways. To execute a single line, place your cursor on that line and press Ctrl+Enter on Windows or Cmd+Enter on Mac. If you want to run multiple lines at once, highlight the lines you want to run and use the same keyboard shortcut. To run the entire script all at once, press Ctrl+Shift+Enter on Windows or Cmd+Shift+Enter on Mac. These shortcuts make it easy to test and execute your code efficiently.

Watch the output of running the script in the Console.

Understanding R Objects

In R, an object is simply a named piece of data that you create and store in your workspace. If you're new to programming, think of an object as a container that holds something—like a number, a list of names, a dataset, or even a graph. When you run code in R, you're often creating or modifying these objects. For example, if you type x <- 5, you're creating an object named x that stores the number 5. R has different types of objects depending on what kind of data you're working with. These include vectors (lists of values), data frames (tables of data), matrices (grids of numbers), and more. Understanding objects is important because everything you do in R—whether analyzing data, creating plots, or running models—usually involves creating and using these objects.

When you run scripts, you'll create different types of data objects. Primarily we will be creating or reading data frame objects either by typing in data or uploading a csv file for use in this book.

R Code

```r
# Numbers

my_number <- 5

# Text (character strings)

my_text <- "Hello Data Mining"

# Vectors (lists of values)

my_numbers <- c(1, 2, 3, 4, 5)

my_names <- c("Alice", "Bob", "Charlie")

# Data frames (like Excel spreadsheets)

my_data <- data.frame(

name = c("Alice", "Bob", "Charlie"),

age = c(25, 30, 35),

score = c(85, 92, 78)
```

```
)
```

Reading Data Files

Most data analytics work starts with loading data in a preexisting file. These files can be read into R – the most easy way is to use csv files as these have no meta data or formatting (they are clean). Other files such as Excel require special packages to be loaded (see below on definition of a package). After data is loaded several functions allow you to view the data easily to validate the upload before using the data in analytics.

R Code
```
# Reading CSV files

data <- read.csv("mydata.csv")

# Reading Excel files (requires readxl package)

library(readxl)

data <- read_excel("mydata.xlsx")

# Viewing your data

View(data) # Opens data in a new tab

head(data) # Shows first 6 rows

summary(data) # Shows basic statistics
```

Part 4: R Packages

R packages are collections of functions, data, and documentation that extend the basic functionality of R, making it easier to perform specialized types of analysis. You can think of them as add-on toolkits designed for specific tasks, such as data visualization, machine learning, time series analysis, or text mining. Most R packages are open source and are created and shared by members of the global R community, including researchers, developers, and data professionals. These packages are typically hosted on CRAN (the Comprehensive R Archive Network), which is the official repository, but others may also be found on platforms like GitHub. Installing a package is simple: you can use the install.packages("package_name") command in the Console, or you can go to the Packages tab in RStudio and use the interface to search for and install packages. Once installed, packages need to be loaded into your session using the library(package_name) function before you can use their tools.

Installing Packages

You only need to install a package once (downloading it form online source) and then it will live on your local machine (unless you delete the files where it is stored or otherwise alter things).

```
R Code
# Install a single packageinstall.packages("ggplot2")


# Install multiple packagesinstall.packages(c("dplyr", "tidyr",
"caret"))
```

Loading Packages

You need to load packages every time you start RStudio so that they are available in the current working project environment.

```
R Code
# Load a packagelibrary(ggplot2)

# Or multiple packages

library(dplyr)

library(tidyr)

library(caret)
```

Essential Packages for data analytics

Here are some packages often used in data analytics (some of which we will use in labs in coming chapters).

- **dplyr**: Data manipulation (filtering, sorting, summarizing)
- **ggplot2**: Creating beautiful visualizations
- **caret**: Machine learning and classification
- **randomForest**: Random forest algorithms
- **e1071**: Support vector machines and other ML algorithms
- **cluster**: Clustering analysis
- **arules**: Association rule mining

- **rpart**: Decision trees

Part 5: Common Script Patterns

When working with R scripts, you typically start by loading your dataset—for example, from a CSV file—and then perform a quick exploration to understand its size, column names, structure, and summary statistics. In R, many operations you perform are done using functions, which are like little machines or tools that take some input, process it, and give you an output. For example, read.csv() is a function that reads data from a CSV file and loads it into R. Functions always have a name followed by parentheses, where you put any information they need, called arguments. Here's how you might load data and explore it:

```
R Code
# Load data


data <- read.csv("sales_data.csv")


# Quick exploration


dim(data) # Dimensions (rows, columns)


names(data) # Column names


str(data) # Structure of data


summary(data) # Summary statistics
```

When working with data frames (tables), you can use the $ operator to access specific columns by name. For example, data$price refers to the "price" column inside the dataset, letting you analyze or plot that specific variable.

In R, functions are individual commands or tools that perform specific tasks, such as calculating a mean or creating a plot. On the other hand, packages are collections of related functions and datasets bundled together to extend R's capabilities. Think of packages as toolkits or libraries that you install and load when you want extra features beyond base R. For example, the ggplot2 package contains many functions specifically designed for advanced data visualization.

After loading and exploring data, you often use functions to create simple visualizations or calculate basic statistics. For example, plot() creates a scatterplot, hist() creates a histogram, and mean() calculates the average value of a variable. Here are some examples:

```R
# Create simple plots

# Scatter plot of price vs. quantity
plot(data$price, data$quantity)

hist(data$price) # Histogram of price

# Basic statistics

mean(data$price) # Mean price

median(data$price) # Median price

table(data$category) # Frequency count of categories
```

Part 6: Tips for Success

Set Your Working Directory

In R, the working directory is the folder on your computer where R looks for files to read and where it saves files by default. It's important to set your working directory to the location where your data files are stored so that you can easily load and save files without typing long file paths. You can set the working directory in R using the setwd() function with the path to your folder, for example:

```
R Code
setwd("C:/Users/YourName/Documents/DataMining").
```

Alternatively, if you're using RStudio, you can set it through the menu by going to the menu bar and Session → Set Working Directory → Choose Directory and selecting the appropriate folder. Setting your working directory correctly helps keep your projects organized and makes working with data files smoother.

File Management

When working in R, it's important to regularly save your progress to avoid losing any of your code or data. The scripts you write in R, which contain your R code, can be saved by pressing Ctrl+S on Windows or Cmd+S on a Mac. These script files usually have the extension .R. Saving your script means your code is safely stored on your computer and can be opened, edited, or run again later without starting from scratch.

Beyond saving scripts, R has something called a workspace, which you can think of as the current memory of your R session. The workspace holds all the data objects, variables, and functions you have created during your work.

Saving the workspace means saving everything you've done so far so that when you come back later, you don't have to reload or recreate all your data and settings — you can pick up exactly where you left off.

To keep everything related to a specific analysis or project organized, RStudio offers a helpful feature called Projects. A project bundles together all your scripts, data files, workspace, and any other documents into a single folder. This way, when you open a project, all the files and information you need for that particular task are in one place. This organization is especially useful if you are working on multiple assignments or analyses at the same time because it prevents files from getting mixed up or lost.

You can create a new project easily in RStudio by going to File → New Project. Using projects helps make your workflow smoother and your work more manageable. So, in summary, regularly save your .R scripts to keep your code safe, save your workspace to keep your data and variables intact, and use RStudio projects to keep everything related to your work well-organized.

Getting Help

When you're working in R, it's common to need help understanding what a function does or how to use it. A strength of R is the well written internal help support system. One way to get help is by typing commands directly in the Console. For example, if you want to learn about the mean() function, you can type ?mean and press Enter, and R will show the documentation for that function. Similarly, if you want to search for help on a topic or keyword, like "clustering," you can type ??clustering to find all related help pages.

In addition to these commands, RStudio provides a very useful Help pane located in the bottom-right corner of the interface. This Help pane allows you to search for functions, packages, and topics without needing to remember the exact commands. You can simply type a keyword or function name into the search box, and relevant help files and guides will appear for you to browse. Clicking on any of these entries will open detailed documentation, including examples of how to use the function, explanations of its arguments, and additional resources.

Using both the help commands (? and ??) in the Console and the Help pane in RStudio gives you quick and easy access to the information you need, making it much easier to learn and troubleshoot as you work with R.

Common Errors and Solutions

As you run script in R the Console will have error messages. Get familiar with what these mean in case you need to trouble shoot.

Error: "Object not found"

- Solution: Make sure you've run the code that creates the object

- Check spelling and capitalization (R is case-sensitive)

Error: "Package not found"

- Solution: Install the package first with install.packages("packagename")

Error: "Cannot find file"

- Solution: Check your working directory and file path

- Use getwd() to see current directory

Best Practices for Script Users

When working with scripts, start by reading the comments—these are lines beginning with # that often explain what each part of the code does. Avoid running the entire script all at once right away; instead, run it section by section to better understand how it works and catch errors early. As you go, check the Environment pane to confirm that variables and objects are being created as expected. Keep your data files well-organized by placing them in the same folder as your scripts, which helps avoid file path issues. Finally, always make a backup copy of the original script before making any changes, so you can easily revert if needed.

Lab 2

Tokenization and Stopword Removal

In this lab, you'll learn how to get raw text ready for analysis by focusing on two important steps: tokenization and removing stopwords. Tokenization means breaking the text into smaller pieces, usually words or sentences, which makes it easier to work with. Once the text is split up, we take out stopwords—common words like "the," "is," or "in" that don't add much meaning. These steps help clean up the text, cutting down on unnecessary noise so it's ready for tasks like counting word frequencies or uncovering topics.

Lesson Steps

Step 1: Setup

Start by installing and loading the packages needed.

```
R Code
# Install if not already installed


options(repos = c(CRAN = "https://cran.r-project.org"))
install.packages(c("tidyverse", "tidytext", "tokenizers"))
library(tidyverse)
library(tidytext)
library(tokenizers)
library(dplyr)
```

Create a simple example to use for the first part of the lab.

```
R Code
text <- tibble(
  id = 1,
  text = "Tokenization is a critical
              first step in NLP. It helps break
              down and analyze text effectively."
)
```

Step 2: Word Tokenization

Next, we'll split the text into single words by using the unnest_tokens() function from the tidytext package. Breaking text down this way, called word tokenization, is a common step for tasks such as counting how often each word appears.

R Code

```
word_tokens <- unnest_tokens(text, output = word,
                             input = text)
print(word_tokens)
```

Output

```
## # A tibble: 16 x 2
##       id word
##    <dbl> <chr>
## 1      1 tokenization
## 2      1 is
## 3      1 a
## 4      1 critical
## 5      1 first
## 6      1 step
## 7      1 in
## 8      1 nlp
## 9      1 it
## 10     1 helps
## 11     1 break
## 12     1 down
## 13     1 and
## 14     1 analyze
## 15     1 text
## 16     1 effectively
```

This returns a list of words in lowercase. This tokenizer also handles basic punctuation but may not manage contractions or hyphenated words.

Step 3: Sentence Tokenization

When you need to analyze sentence-level features like sentiment or gram-mar, it's helpful to break the text into sentences. You can do this using the tokenize_sentences() function from the tokenizers package:

```
R Code
library(tokenizers)

text <- "Dogs bark. Cats meow."
tokenize_sentences(text)[[1]]
```

```
Output
## [1] "Dogs bark." "Cats meow."
```

The text was split into two sentences. Be aware that sentence splitting may have limitations when working with abbreviations like "U.S." or titles like "Dr."

Step 4: Stopword Removal – Setup

Now let's move on to stopword removal. Stopwords are common words that do not contribute meaning to NLP analysis.

Here is a new example using the classic sentence that contains every letter of the alphabet:

```
R Code
text_data <- data.frame(
  text = "The quick brown fox jumps over the lazy dog")
```

Step 5: Tokenize the Sentence

Tokenize the sentence into words with `unnest_tokens()`. Each word will appear split and have its own row in the resulting data frame.

R Code
```
tokens <- unnest_tokens(text_data, output = word, input = text)
print(tokens)
```

Output
```
##      word
## 1     the
## 2   quick
## 3   brown
## 4     fox
## 5   jumps
## 6    over
## 7     the
## 8    lazy
## 9     dog
```

Step 6: Remove Stopwords

After that, we'll get rid of common stopwords by using the stopword list that comes with tidytext. The anti_join() function helps us filter out any words that appear on that list.

R Code

```
data("stop_words")
cleaned_tokens <- anti_join(tokens, stop_words,
                            by = "word")
```

This will filter out words like "the" and "over" so you are left meaningful terms.

Step 7: View Cleaned Tokens

Let's look at what remains after stopword removal:

R Code

```
print(cleaned_tokens)
```

Output

```
##     word
## 1 quick
## 2 brown
## 3   fox
## 4 jumps
## 5  lazy
## 6   dog
```

You should now see words like "quick," "brown," "fox," "jumps," "lazy," and "dog"—terms that better reflect the content of the sentence.

Step 8: Customize Stopword List (Optional)

At times, the standard stopword lists can be too aggressive and remove words you actually want to keep. For instance, if you want to include the word "over" in your analysis, you can customize the stopword list to leave it in. Here's how you can do that:

```
R Code
custom_stopwords <- filter(stop_words, word != "over")
tokens_no_not <- anti_join(tokens, custom_stopwords,
                           by = "word")
print(tokens_no_not)
```

```
Output
##     word
## 1 quick
## 2 brown
## 3   fox
## 4 jumps
## 5  over
## 6  lazy
## 7   dog
```

Now, the word "over" will remain in your results. This is especially helpful in sentiment analysis, where small words can change the meaning of an entire sentence.

Wrap-Up

In this lab, you practiced two core text preprocessing techniques: tokenization and stopword removal. Tokenization allows us to break down raw text into manageable pieces, while stopword removal filters out common words that may not contribute meaningful insight. These steps are foundational in nearly every text mining or natural language processing task, helping to clean and structure textual data before deeper analysis. Depending on your goal—such as topic modeling, classification, or sentiment analysis—you can tailor how much preprocessing to apply, including customizing your stopword lists.

Exercises

Tokenization and Stopword Removal

In this exercise you will practice tokenizing text into words and sentences, and removing stopwords to clean the data for analysis.

Dataset 1: Simple Product Reviews

```
R Code
reviews <- tibble(
id = 1:3,
text = c(
"I love this phone! Camera is amazing, battery life is great.",
"Terrible customer service. It stopped working after a week.",
"Decent quality for the price. Not the best, but okay overall."
  )
)
```

1. Break down the `reviews` column into individual words using `unnest_tokens()` and display the tokens you get.
2. Next, split the same text into sentences with the `tokenize_sentences()` function and show the sentence-level tokens.
3. Use `anti_join()` along with the `stop_words` dataset to filter out common English stopwords from the word tokens. Present the cleaned list of tokens.
4. Count how many tokens remain in the entire dataset after removing stopwords and share the total number.
5. Build a custom stopword list that keeps the word "not," which is often removed by default. Apply this updated list to remove stopwords and compare the resulting tokens to those from the standard stopword

removal.

Dataset 2: Tweets About a Movie

```
R Code
tweets <- tibble(
  tweet_id = 1:4,
  text = c(
    "Just watched the new movie! Absolutely loved it. #cinema",
    "The movie was okay, but I expected more by the director.",
    "Not a fan of the storyline, but the acting was decent.",
    "Best movie I've seen all year! Highly recommend it."
  )
)
```

6. Break the tweets down into individual words and display the tokens.
7. Remove stopwords from these tweet tokens and show the remaining words.
8. For the tweet with `tweet_id = 3`, count how many words remain after stopwords are removed and share the number.
9. Tokenize the tweets into sentences. How many sentences does the tweet with `tweet_id = 1` contain?
10. Explain briefly why it might be useful to either keep or remove hashtags (words starting with #) when tokenizing tweets. Write 2 to 3 sentences.

Dataset 3: News Headlines

```
R Code
headlines <- tibble(
  headline_id = 1:3,
  headline = c(
    "Government passes new climate change legislation",
    "Local sports team wins championship after intense final",
    "Economy shows signs of recovery, experts say"
  )
)
```

11. Tokenize the headlines into words and remove stopwords. Show the final cleaned tokens.

12. Create a frequency table of the cleaned tokens across all headlines. Which token appears most frequently?

Lab 3

Stemming and Lemmatization

Stemming and lemmatization are two popular methods in natural language processing for simplifying words down to their basic forms, a process often called text normalization. Stemming is a quick and straightforward approach that chops off word endings using fixed rules, without considering grammar or meaning. It's handy for applications like search engines, where matching different word forms is enough, though it can sometimes produce stems that aren't actual words.

Lemmatization takes a different approach by relying on dictionaries and grammatical rules to find the proper root form, or lemma, of a word. This makes it a bit slower but much more precise. It's especially useful when the true meaning and correct form of words matter, like in chatbots or translation systems. In this lab, you'll explore how both methods work and when you might choose one over the other.

Lesson Steps

Step 1: Setting Up

Before starting, let's make sure we have the necessary packages installed and ready. We'll use textstem for lemmatizing words, SnowballC for stemming, and tm for common text mining tasks such as building corpora and removing stopwords. Once installed, we'll load these libraries so we can use their functions throughout the lab.

```
R Code
# Install if not already installed


options(repos = c(CRAN = "https://cran.r-project.org"))
install.packages("textstem")
install.packages("tm")
install.packages("SnowballC")


library(textstem)
library(tm)
library(SnowballC)
```

Step 2: Creating a List of Words

Next, create a sample list of words that includes various forms.

```
R Code
words <- c(
  "running", "runs", "easily", "fairly",
  "children", "better", "connection",
  "connections"
)
```

Step 3: Performing Stemming with the Porter Stemmer

Stemming works by trimming common endings off words to get their root form. It doesn't rely on dictionaries or consider the word's grammatical role. In this lab, we'll use the wordStem() function from the SnowballC package, which applies the Porter stemming algorithm by default.

R Code

```
stemmed_words <- wordStem(words, language = "en")
stem_output <- data.frame(
  Original = words,
  Stemmed = stemmed_words
)
print(stem_output)
```

Output

```
##         Original  Stemmed
## 1        running      run
## 2          runs      run
## 3        easily   easili
## 4        fairly     fair
## 5      children children
## 6        better   better
## 7   connection  connect
## 8  connections  connect
```

This creates a table that shows the original words next to their stemmed forms. Notice that some results—like "easily" becoming "easili"—aren't real

31

words. This highlights a major limitation of stemming.

Step 4: Performing Lemmatization with `textstem`

Next, we'll explore lemmatization, which turns words into their proper dictionary forms by applying vocabulary and grammar rules. For this, we'll use the lemmatize_words() function from the textstem package.

```
R Code
lemmatized_words <- lemmatize_words(words)
lemm_output <- data.frame(
  Original = words,
  Lemmatized = lemmatized_words
)
print(lemm_output)
```

```
Output
##        Original Lemmatized
## 1       running        run
## 2          runs        run
## 3        easily     easily
## 4        fairly     fairly
## 5      children      child
## 6        better       good
## 7    connection connection
## 8   connections connection
```

Usually, lemmatization gives you clear, meaningful words. For instance, it changes "children" to "child" and "better" to "good." These results tend to be more precise and easier to interpret compared to what stemming produces.

Step 5: Comparing Stemming and Lemmatization Side by Side

To clearly see the difference between the two techniques, we can place both results in a single comparison table:

R Code

```
comparison <- data.frame(
  Original = words,
  Stemmed = wordStem(words),
  Lemmatized = lemmatize_words(words)
)
print(comparison)
```

Output

```
##       Original  Stemmed Lemmatized
## 1      running      run        run
## 2         runs      run        run
## 3       easily   easili     easily
## 4       fairly   fairli     fairly
## 5     children children      child
## 6       better   better       good
## 7   connection  connect connection
## 8  connections  connect connection
```

Take a close look at the differences. The stemmer cuts "connections" down to "connect," while the lemmatizer keeps it as "connection." With "children," the stemmer doesn't really help, but the lemmatizer correctly returns "child." These examples highlight how lemmatization understands language better, though it usually takes more time to process.

Wrap-Up

In this lab, you worked with two techniques for reducing words to a simpler form: stemming and lemmatization. Stemming is quick and useful when exact accuracy isn't a priority, though it can produce rough or incorrect word forms. Lemmatization takes longer but gives cleaner, more meaningful results by using grammar and vocabulary. Which method you choose depends on what your analysis needs—whether you're aiming for speed and broad matching, or more precise, language-aware output. Knowing the difference is key when building effective text processing workflows.

Exercises

Stemming and Lemmatization In this exercise, you'll get hands-on practice with two core techniques for normalizing text: stemming and lemmatization. Stemming works by quickly trimming word endings, often producing rough stems that aren't actual words. Lemmatization, on the other hand, uses grammar and vocabulary rules to return meaningful root forms. You'll try both methods on different text examples to see how they behave and what sets them apart.

Dataset 1: Mixed Word Forms

```
R Code
words1 <- c(
  "running", "runs", "easily", "fairly",
  "children", "better", "connection", "connections"
)
```

1. Apply the Porter stemmer using `wordStem()` to the `words1` list. Display the original words alongside their stemmed versions.
2. Use the `lemmatize_words()` function to lemmatize the same `words1` list. Show the original words next to their lemmatized forms.
3. Combine your results into one table that compares each original word with both its stemmed and lemmatized versions.
4. Identify any words that the Porter stemmer transforms into something that isn't a real word. List those results.
5. Find the words where lemmatization changes the original word into a different, correct form. List those as well.

Dataset 2: Sentences With Variations of Verbs and Nouns

R Code
```
sentences <- c(
  "The cats are running swiftly in the gardens.",
  "He studies the connections between different networks.",
  "Better understanding leads to easier problem solving."
)
```

6. Break the sentences into individual words using `unnest_tokens()` from the tidytext package.
7. Apply the Porter stemmer to all tokens and display the first 10 results.
8. Use `lemmatize_words()` to lemmatize the tokens and show the first 10 lemmatized words.
9. Look at how the word "connections" is handled by both methods. What's the difference between the stemmed and lemmatized versions?
10. In a few sentences, explain why lemmatization might be a better choice than stemming for tasks where grammar and word accuracy matter.

Dataset 3: Product Descriptions

R Code
```
descriptions <- c(
descriptions <- c(
  "Long battery life and fast performance.",
  "Smooth updates and better camera.",
  "Fast delivery, perfect condition.",
  "Great speed and battery power.",
  "Users love the new features."
)
)
```

11. Tokenize the product descriptions into words, then stem and lemmatize these tokens. Show a side-by-side comparison table for the first 15 tokens.

12. Based on your observations, which normalization method (stemming or lemmatization) better preserves the meaning of words in product descriptions? Provide a brief explanation.

Lab 4

Regular Expressions (Regex) for Text Cleaning

Regular expressions, or regex, are a powerful way to find and work with patterns in text. They're especially helpful when dealing with unstructured or messy data that needs cleaning before analysis. In this lab, you'll use the stringr package in R to apply regex techniques for cleaning up text, pulling out useful details, and making input more consistent.

Lesson Steps

Step 1: Load Required Package

Install and loading the `stringr` package, which provides functions for string manipulation using regex patterns.

```
R Code
# Install if not already installed
options(repos = c(CRAN = "https://cran.r-project.org"))
install.packages("stringr")
library(stringr)
```

Step 2: Remove Special Characters and Punctuation

One common step in cleaning text is to strip out everything except letters, numbers, and spaces. This gets rid of extra clutter like punctuation, hashtags, and other symbols. The str_replace_all() function is useful for this—it finds patterns in the text and replaces them, usually with nothing, to tidy things up.

```
R Code
text <- "Wow!!! This product is amazing :) #loveit"
clean_text <- str_replace_all(text, "[^A-Za-z0-9 ]", "")
print(clean_text)
```

```
Output
## [1] "Wow This product is amazing  loveit"
```

The pattern [^A-Za-z0-9] matches any character that is not a letter, digit, or space, and removes it.

Step 3: Extract Structured Patterns

Regex can also be used to pull out useful pieces of text, like an email address, phone number, or date. The str_extract() function helps with this by returning the first part of the string that matches your pattern.

For example, the pattern below captures a typical email address by looking for a username, followed by the at symbol, and then a domain name.

R Code
```
text2 <- "Please contact us at support@example.com"


email <- str_extract(
  text2,
  "[\\w\\.\\-]+@[\\w\\.\\-]+\\.[a-zA-Z]{2,}"
)
print(email)
```

Output
```
## [1] "support@example.com"
```

This matches a phone number in the format (123) 456-7890.

R Code
```
text3<-"or call (123) 456-7890 by 05/11/2025."
phone <- str_extract(text3, "\\(\\d{3}\\) \\d{3}-\\d{4}")
print(phone)
```

Output
```
## [1] "(123) 456-7890"
```

This matches a date in the format MM/DD/YYYY.

R Code
```
date <- str_extract(text3, "\\d{2}/\\d{2}/\\d{4}")
print(date)
```

Output

```
## [1] "05/11/2025"
```

Step 4: Remove Extra Spaces

Text can sometimes include extra spaces between words, which makes it harder to work with. The pattern \s+ matches any group of whitespace characters, like spaces or tabs. Using str_replace_all(), you can replace those with a single space to clean things up.

R Code

```
messy <- "This     sentence     has     too     many     spaces."
cleaned <- str_replace_all(messy, "\\s+", " ")
print(cleaned)
```

Output

```
## [1] "This sentence has too many spaces."
```

This results in evenly spaced text, which is easier to read and analyze.

Step 5: Anonymize URLs

To protect user privacy or simplify data, we can replace web URLs with a placeholder. The pattern https?://\\S+ matches a full URL starting with http:// or https:// followed by any non-space characters.

R Code

```
text3 <- "Visit our site at https://example.com for more info."
anonymized <- str_replace_all(text3, "https?://\\S+", "[URL]")
print(anonymized)
```

Output

```
## [1] "Visit our site at [URL] for more info."
```

This replaces the actual URL with [URL], making the text cleaner and anonymized.

Wrap-Up

In this lab, you explored how to use regex in R to handle common text-cleaning tasks. You practiced removing unnecessary characters, pulling out useful patterns, tidying up formatting, and masking sensitive data. These basic techniques are essential for getting raw text ready for deeper analysis.

Exercises

Regular Expressions (Regex) for Text Cleaning

In this exercise, you will practice using regular expressions (regex) in R to clean and extract useful information from text data.

Dataset 1: Social Media Posts

```
R Code
posts <- c(
  "Visit https://amazing-product.com #awesome :)",
  "Contact jane.doe@example.org or call (555) 123-4567",
  "Big sale from 07/15/2025 - don't miss it!!!  "
)
```

1. Use `str_replace_all()` with a regex pattern to strip out all punctuation and special characters from the `posts`, leaving only letters, numbers, and spaces. Display the cleaned version.

2. Pull out any URLs in the text using `str_extract()`. What links were found?

3. Search for phone numbers that follow the format `(xxx) xxx-xxxx` and show the matches.

4. Look for any dates written as MM/DD/YYYY in the `posts` and display the ones that were found.

5. Clean up the text by removing any extra spaces so that only single spaces remain between words. Show the updated version.

Dataset 2: Customer Support Messages

```
R Code
messages <- c(
  "My email is user123@gmail.com; please respond!",
  "The support number is (800) 555-9876. Thanks!",
  "Our meeting is scheduled for 12/01/2024. "
)
```

6. Extract all email addresses from the messages dataset using regex.
7. Extract phone numbers matching the pattern (xxx) xxx-xxxx from messages.
8. Extract dates in MM/DD/YYYY format from the messages.
9. Replace all URLs in the following vector with [URL]:

```
R Code
urls <- c("Visit http://example.com",
    "Secure site: https://secure.example.com/login")
```

10. Show the anonymized text. Explain why anonymizing URLs or other sensitive data might be important when preparing text data for analysis.

Dataset 3: Mixed Text Entries

```
R Code
entries <- c(
  "Call (123) 456-7890 or email contact@company.net.",
  "Launch: 09/30/2025. Check https://launch.example.com .",
  "Thanks!!!    This is great :-)    "
)
```

11. Use regex to replace URLs in `entries` with `[URL]`. Show the cleaned entries.

12. Use regex to remove special characters and extra spaces from `entries`. Show the cleaned text.

Lab 5

Bag of Words (Encoding)

Text data must be transformed into numerical representations before it can be used in statistical models or machine learning (a process known as encoding). One of the most straightforward ways to do this is through a Bag of Words (BoW) approach. In a BoW each document is represented by a vector that counts how many times each word appears. This method ignores grammar and word order, but it's simple and effective for many text classification problems. In this lab, you'll build a BoW representation.

Lesson Steps

Step 1: Setup

First, install and load the packages needed.

R Code
```
# Install if not already installed
options(repos = c(CRAN = "https://cran.r-project.org"))
install.packages(c("tidytext", "dplyr", "tidyr", "tibble"))
library(tidytext)
library(dplyr)
library(tidyr)
library(tibble)
```

Create a small set of three sample documents stored in a tibble.

R Code
```
docs <- tibble(
  doc_id = 1:3,
  text = c("I like apples",
           "I like oranges",
           "I like bananas")
)
docs
```

Output
```
## # A tibble: 3 x 2
##   doc_id text
##    <int> <chr>
## 1      1 I like apples
## 2      2 I like oranges
## 3      3 I like bananas
```

This prints a table of your sample documents. Each row is one document. A collection of documents is called a Corpus in NLP.

Step 2: Tokenization

Before analyzing text, it's important to split the full text into separate words—a step known as tokenization. The unnest_tokens() function from the tidytext package simplifies this by turning each document into a tidy format where every row contains just one word from that document. This makes the data easier to work with for further analysis.

```
R Code
tokenized <- unnest_tokens(docs, word, text)
tokenized
```

```
Output
## # A tibble: 9 x 2
##   doc_id word
##    <int> <chr>
## 1      1 i
## 2      1 like
## 3      1 apples
## 4      2 i
## 5      2 like
## 6      2 oranges
## 7      3 i
## 8      3 like
## 9      3 bananas
```

Once this is done, your data will be arranged in a long format, with each word from every document occupying its own row. This layout makes it simpler to count, group, and analyze words across the entire collection of documents.

Step 3: Create the Bag of Words

With the words tokenized, the next step is to find out how many times each word shows up in each document. Using the count() function from dplyr, you can create a summary table that includes three columns: doc_id, word, and n, which tells you the frequency of each word within its document.

```
R Code
word_counts <- count(tokenized, doc_id, word)
word_counts
```

```
Output
## # A tibble: 9 x 3
##    doc_id word          n
##     <int> <chr>     <int>
## 1       1 apples        1
## 2       1 i             1
## 3       1 like          1
## 4       2 i             1
## 5       2 like          1
## 6       2 oranges       1
## 7       3 bananas       1
## 8       3 i             1
## 9       3 like          1
```

Next, we transform this long-format data into a wide-format document-term matrix using pivot_wider() from tidyr. In this matrix, each row corresponds to a document, and each column represents a word. The values in the cells show how many times each word occurs in each document. This setup is the core idea behind the Bag of Words model.

R Code

```
bow_matrix <- pivot_wider(word_counts, names_from = word,
                          values_from = n, values_fill = 0)
bow_matrix
```

Output

```
## # A tibble: 3 x 6
##    doc_id apples     i  like oranges bananas
##     <int>  <int> <int> <int>   <int>   <int>
## 1       1      1     1     1       0       0
## 2       2      0     1     1       1       0
## 3       3      0     1     1       0       1
```

At this point, you now have a complete Bag of Words in standard matrix form—documents as rows, words as columns, and word counts as values. However, this format is often inefficient for a computer to use due to the large number of zeros it contains.

Step 4: Convert to Sparse Matrix (Final Result)

In most real-world datasets, each document only uses a small portion of all the words in the vocabulary. Because of this, the Bag of Words matrix created earlier ends up with lots of zeros, which takes up unnecessary memory and can slow things down.

To handle this, we turn the matrix into a sparse format that only keeps track of the non-zero values. This makes the Bag of Words model much more efficient and practical.

First the wide-format bow_matrix (without the document ID column) gets converted into a standard numeric matrix. After that, we use the Matrix package to change it into a sparse matrix.

```R
library(Matrix)


regular_matrix <- as.matrix(bow_matrix[, -1])
sparse_mat <- as(regular_matrix, "sparseMatrix")
sparse_mat
```

```
## 3 x 5 sparse Matrix of class "dgCMatrix"
##      apples i like oranges bananas
## [1,]      1 1    1       .       .
## [2,]      . 1    1       1       .
## [3,]      . 1    1       .       1
```

This final output is a sparse document-term matrix —a memory-efficient, ready-to-use representation of your text data. It is the complete and final result of the Bag of Words process and can be the input for further NLP work.

Wrap-Up

The Bag of Words method offers a straightforward way to represent text by turning documents into vectors that count how often each word appears. This makes it easy to plug text data into many modeling techniques. That said, BoW has its drawbacks—it doesn't capture the order of words or their

meanings, and the matrix can grow huge when dealing with large vocabular-
ies. Despite these limitations, it's still a solid starting point for text analysis,
especially when combined with methods like removing stop words or applying TF-IDF weighting, which we'll explore in later labs.

Exercises

Bag of Words (Encoding)

In this exercise set, you will practice converting text data into numeric representations using the Bag of Words (BoW) approach.

Dataset 1: Short Customer Feedbacks

```
R Code
feedback <- tibble(
  doc_id = 1:4,
  text = c(
    "The product is excellent and easy to use",
    "I found the product difficult to use",
    "Excellent value for the price",
    "Not satisfied with the product quality"
  )
)
```

1. Break down the `feedback` dataset into individual words by applying `unnest_tokens()`.
2. Count the frequency of each word within every document and display the table.
3. Transform the data into a wide-format Bag of Words matrix where each row represents a document and each column shows word counts.
4. Convert this Bag of Words matrix—excluding the `doc_id` column—into a standard numeric matrix.
5. Use the `Matrix` package to turn the numeric matrix into a sparse matrix and then display a summary of it.

Dataset 2: Movie Reviews

```
R Code
reviews <- tibble(
  doc_id = 1:10,
text <- c(
  "Loved the acting",
  "Boring and too long",
  "Great music, weak plot",
  "Amazing visuals, okay story",
  "Terrible pacing, dull scenes",
  "Engaging and well-acted",
  "Predictable but fun",
  "Too slow to enjoy",
  "Fantastic cast, bad ending",
  "Good story, poor editing"
)
)
```

6. Break the `reviews` dataset into individual words using tokenization.
7. Count how often each word appears in each document.
8. Build a wide Bag of Words matrix where each row is a document and columns are word counts.
9. Find out which word has the highest total frequency across all documents by summing counts for each word.
10. Convert the Bag of Words matrix into a sparse matrix format.

Dataset 3: Product Descriptions

```
R Code
products <- tibble(
  doc_id = 1:6,
  text = c(
    "Wireless noise-canceling headphones",
    "GPS smartwatch monitor",
    "Compact Bluetooth speaker",
    "Fast charging cable",
    "Portable power bank",
    "Smart home sensor"
  )
)
```

11. Tokenize and create a Bag of Words wide matrix for products.
12. Explain in 2-3 sentences the advantage of using sparse matrices when working with Bag of Words models on large text datasets.

Lab 6

TF-IDF: Term Frequency–Inverse Document Frequency

TF-IDF is a technique used in text analysis to highlight the most important words within a document. It blends two concepts: term frequency (TF), which counts how often a word shows up in a specific document, and inverse document frequency (IDF), which lowers the weight of words that appear across many documents. By combining these, TF-IDF helps pinpoint words that are significant in one document but not widespread throughout the whole collection. This method is often applied in search engines, filtering, and classification tasks.

Lesson Steps

Step 1: Setup and Create a Toy Corpus

Before diving in, we first install and load the required R packages.

```
R Code
# Install if not already installed
options(repos = c(CRAN = "https://cran.r-project.org"))


# Install required packages (only run once)
install.packages(c("tidytext", "dplyr", "tibble", "tidyr"))


# Load libraries
library(tidytext)
library(dplyr)
library(tibble)
library(tidyr)
```

Let's create a small dataset containing three short documents, each made up of a sentence listing different fruit names.

```
R Code
# Create a small dataset with 3 short documents
documents <- tibble(
  document = c("doc1", "doc2", "doc3"),
  text = c("apple orange apple",
           "orange banana apple",
           "banana orange banana")
)


documents
```

```
Output
## # A tibble: 3 x 2
##   document text
##   <chr>    <chr>
## 1 doc1     apple orange apple
## 2 doc2     orange banana apple
## 3 doc3     banana orange banana
```

After running this code, we have a data frame with two columns: the document name and its text. Each row represents one document.

Step 2: Tokenize and Count Words

To get the text ready for analysis, we split it into individual words using the unnest_tokens() function—a process known as tokenization. This way, each word ends up in its own row along with the document it belongs to. After that, we use the count() function to tally how often each word appears within each document.

```
R Code
# Break text into individual words (tokens)
tokenized <- unnest_tokens(documents, word, text)


# Count how often each word appears in each document
word_counts <- count(tokenized, document, word, sort = TRUE)


# View the result
word_counts
```

```
Output
## # A tibble: 7 x 3
##    document word        n
##    <chr>    <chr>   <int>
## 1 doc1     apple       2
## 2 doc3     banana      2
## 3 doc1     orange      1
## 4 doc2     apple       1
## 5 doc2     banana      1
## 6 doc2     orange      1
## 7 doc3     orange      1
```

This produces a table where each row shows a word, the document it came from, and the number of times that word appears in that document. This forms the basis for calculating TF-IDF.

Step 3: Calculate TF-IDF Scores

With the word counts in hand, the next step is to calculate the TF-IDF score for each word within each document. This transforms simple counts into values that show how important a word is in one document compared to the entire collection. We do this using the bind_tf_idf() function from the tidytext package, which takes the counts and adds columns for term frequency (TF), inverse document frequency (IDF), and the overall TF-IDF score.

R Code

```
# Calculate TF-IDF values
tfidf <- bind_tf_idf(word_counts, word, document, n)


# View the result
tfidf
```

Output

```
## # A tibble: 7 x 6
##    document word       n    tf   idf tf_idf
##    <chr>    <chr>  <int> <dbl> <dbl>  <dbl>
## 1 doc1      apple      2 0.667 0.405  0.270
## 2 doc3      banana     2 0.667 0.405  0.270
## 3 doc1      orange     1 0.333 0      0
## 4 doc2      apple      1 0.333 0.405  0.135
## 5 doc2      banana     1 0.333 0.405  0.135
## 6 doc2      orange     1 0.333 0      0
## 7 doc3      orange     1 0.333 0      0
```

The result is a new table that shows not just the counts but also the TF, IDF, and TF-IDF scores. Words like "apple" in "doc1" and "banana" in "doc3" receive higher scores because they appear frequently in one document but not in all documents, marking them as important yet uncommon words. This shows how TFIDF helps us focus on words that are more informative and specific to each document.

61

Step 4: Compare TF-IDF to Bag of Words

At this point, the TF-IDF matrix is complete. Unlike the Bag of Words method, which simply counts how many times each word appears, the TF-IDF version adjusts the scores based on how common or rare a word is across all documents. For example, the word "orange" appears in all three documents, so its TF-IDF score will be low. But the word "banana" appears mostly in "doc3", so it will get a higher score there.

Wrap-Up

In this lab, we showed how to convert plain text into a weighted matrix using TF-IDF, which balances how often words appear with how unique they are across documents. We began with a simple collection of documents, broke the text into individual words, and counted their frequencies. Then, we used the bind_tf_idf() function to calculate scores that highlight important words in each document while lowering the impact of common words found everywhere. Unlike raw counts, TF-IDF offers a clearer way to spot keywords that truly define each document. This makes it a powerful approach for tasks like search indexing, classifying documents, and filtering out common but uninformative terms.

Exercises

TF-IDF: Term Frequency–Inverse Document Frequency

In this exercise you will practice calculating TF-IDF scores to find important words in documents.

Dataset 1: Simple Animal Descriptions

```
R Code
animals <- tibble(
  document = c("doc1", "doc2", "doc3"),
  text = c("cat dog cat",
           "dog bird cat",
           "bird bird dog")
)
```

1. Break the `animals` dataset into individual words by applying `unnest_tokens()`.
2. Count the frequency of each word within every document.
3. Use `bind_tf_idf()` to calculate the TF-IDF scores for each word in each document.
4. Identify which word in `doc1` has the highest TF-IDF score and show that result.
5. Briefly explain why the TF-IDF score for "dog" might be lower than for "cat" in `doc1`.

Dataset 2: Tech Product Reviews

```
R Code
tech_reviews <- tibble(
  document = c("review1", "review2", "review3"),
  text = c("fast processor and great battery life",
           "battery life is poor but the screen is bright",
           "great screen and fast processor")
)
```

6. Tokenize the `tech_reviews` dataset into words.
7. Count word frequencies per document.
8. Calculate TF-IDF scores for the words.
9. Identify the word with the highest TF-IDF score in `review2` and explain what this indicates.

Dataset 3: Travel Blog Posts

```
R Code
travel_posts <- tibble(
  document = c("post1", "post2", "post3"),
  text = c("exploring the beaches and mountains",
           "mountains offer breathtaking views and hiking",
           "beaches are perfect for relaxation and swimming")
)
```

10. Tokenize and count words per document.
11. Calculate TF-IDF scores for the travel posts dataset.
12. Compare the TF-IDF scores of "beaches" and "mountains" in `post3`. Which has the higher score and why?

Lab 7

Word and Contextual Embeddings

Introduction

Word embeddings turn words into numbers in a way that captures their meaning and how they're used. Unlike older methods like bag-of-words or TF-IDF, which just count how often words appear, embeddings reflect both meaning and context. Words that appear in similar ways or situations end up with similar vector representations. For instance, the model might learn that the difference between "king" and "man" is a lot like the difference between "queen" and "woman."

In this lab, we'll explore word embeddings using the GloVe algorithm—a popular approach that learns word meanings by analyzing patterns in large text corpora. We'll also introduce the idea of contextual embeddings to see how a word's meaning can shift based on how it's used.

Lesson Steps

Step 1: Install and Load Required Packages

To get started, install and load the packages to use.

```
R Code
# Install if not already installed
options(repos = c(CRAN = "https://cran.r-project.org"))
install.packages("text2vec")
install.packages("data.table")


library(text2vec)
library(data.table)
```

Step 2: Create Sample Text Data

Next, we'll make a small set of example sentences.

```
R Code
text_data <- c(
"I love machine learning and NLP.",
"Text mining and word embeddings are useful for NLP.",
"Deep learning models such as BERT and GPT are popular.")
```

Step 3: Tokenize Text and Create an Iterator

First, we standardize the text by converting all the words to lowercase. This way, words like "Machine" and "machine" are seen as the same. Next, we break down each sentence into individual words, a process called tokenization. To do this, we use itoken(), which creates an iterator that lets the model read and process each word one by one.

R Code

```
tokens <- word_tokenizer(tolower(text_data))


# View the first few tokens from the first text element
print("Sample tokens from first text entry:")
```

Output

```
## [1] "Sample tokens from first text entry:"
```

R Code

```
print(head(tokens[[1]]))
```

Output

```
## [1] "i"          "love"      "machine"   "learning" "and"        "nlp"
```

R Code

```
it <- itoken(tokens, progressbar = FALSE)
```

Step 4: Create and Prune Vocabulary

Next, we build a vocabulary list. This list includes all the words found in the dataset and records how often each word appears. We use `prune_vocabulary()` to filter out any words that appear fewer than a set number of times. Since our sample data is very small here we keep all words by setting the minimum term count to one.

R Code
```
vocab <- create_vocabulary(it)
vocab <- prune_vocabulary(vocab, term_count_min = 1)

# View the size of the vocabulary
cat("Vocabulary size:", nrow(vocab), "\n")
```

Output
```
## Vocabulary size: 20
```

R Code
```
# Show the top 10 most frequent terms
print("Top 10 terms by frequency:")
```

Output
```
## [1] "Top 10 terms by frequency:"
```

R Code
```
print(head(vocab[order(-vocab$term_count), ], 10))
```

Output

```
## Number of docs: 3
## 0 stopwords:  ...
## ngram_min = 1; ngram_max = 1
## Vocabulary:
##               term term_count doc_count
##             <char>     <int>     <int>
##   1:          and         3         3
##   2:          are         2         2
##   3:     learning         2         2
##   4:          nlp         2         2
##   5:           as         1         1
##   6:         bert         1         1
##   7:         deep         1         1
##   8:   embeddings         1         1
##   9:          for         1         1
## 10:          gpt         1         1
```

Step 5: Create the Term Co-occurrence Matrix

Now, we make a table called a term co-occurrence matrix (or TCM). This table shows how often two words show up close to each other in the text. This helps the model understand which words usually hang out together. The skip_grams_window is just a setting that tells us how many words before and after a word we should look at to find its neighbors

R Code

```
vectorizer <- vocab_vectorizer(vocab)
tcm <- create_tcm(it, vectorizer, skip_grams_window = 5)


# Check the dimensions of the TCM
cat("Term Co-occurrence Matrix dimensions:", dim(tcm), "\n")
```

Output

```
## Term Co-occurrence Matrix dimensions: 20 20
```

R Code

```
# View a small portion of the TCM (top-left 5x5 matrix)
print("Sample of the term co-occurrence matrix:")
```

Output

```
## [1] "Sample of the term co-occurrence matrix:"
```

R Code

```
print(as.matrix(tcm[1:5, 1:5]))
```

Output

```
##              as bert deep embeddings        for
## as           0    1 0.25         0 0.0000000
## bert         0    0 0.20         0 0.0000000
## deep         0    0 0.00         0 0.0000000
## embeddings   0    0 0.00         0 0.3333333
## for          0    0 0.00         0 0.0000000
```

Step 6: Train the GloVe Model

Next, we teach the GloVe model using the table of word pairs we made. The model learns to turn each word into a list of 50 numbers that capture its meaning. We run this learning process 10 times to help the model get better.

R Code

```
glove <- GlobalVectors$new(rank = 50, x_max = 10)
word_vectors <- glove$fit_transform(tcm, n_iter = 10)
```

```
Output
## INFO  [14:58:10.484] epoch 1, loss 0.1369
## INFO  [14:58:10.504] epoch 2, loss 0.0852
## INFO  [14:58:10.509] epoch 3, loss 0.0588
## INFO  [14:58:10.511] epoch 4, loss 0.0430
## INFO  [14:58:10.512] epoch 5, loss 0.0327
## INFO  [14:58:10.513] epoch 6, loss 0.0255
## INFO  [14:58:10.514] epoch 7, loss 0.0202
## INFO  [14:58:10.515] epoch 8, loss 0.0163
## INFO  [14:58:10.516] epoch 9, loss 0.0133
## INFO  [14:58:10.517] epoch 10, loss 0.0109
```

Each word is now represented by a numeric vector that reflects its meaning and context in the text. Words that appear in similar contexts will have similar vectors, allowing us to measure how related different words are.

Step 7: Combine Main and Context Vectors

The GloVe model learns two vectors for each word: one for its use as a central word and one for its use in context. We combine them by adding the two vectors together to get the final word embedding for each word.

R Code
```
# Extract the context vectors from the GloVe model
context_vectors <- glove$components


# Combine the main word vectors and the context vectors
word_embeddings <- word_vectors + t(context_vectors)


# View the dimensions of the combined
# word embeddings matrix
cat("Dimensions of word embeddings:",
    dim(word_embeddings), "\n")
```

Output
```
## Dimensions of word embeddings: 20 50
```

R Code
```
# View the first 5 rows and first 5 columns
# of the combined embeddings to inspect values
print("Sample of combined word embeddings:")
```

Output
```
## [1] "Sample of combined word embeddings:"
```

R Code
```
print(round(word_embeddings[1:5, 1:5], 4))
```

```
Output
##               [,1]     [,2]     [,3]     [,4]     [,5]
## as          0.5813   0.0904   0.0078  -0.0434  -0.5597
## bert       -0.0831  -0.3015   0.3846   0.4648   0.5197
## deep        0.6159   0.2020   0.3756  -0.3679  -0.5367
## embeddings  0.1926  -0.3166   0.7726   0.3413   0.5369
## for        -0.4078   0.0205  -0.4285  -0.2954  -0.1568
```

Step 8: Inspect the Word Vector for a Specific Word

Now, we can check out the "embedding" for any word we want. For example, if we look up the word "machine".

R Code

```
# Step 8: Inspect the Word Vector for a Specific Word


# Choose the word to inspect
target_word <- "machine"


# Check if the word exists in the word embeddings matrix
if (target_word %in% rownames(word_embeddings)) {
  cat("First 10 values of word vector for '",
      target_word, "':\n", sep = "")
  # Extract and print the first 5 values,to 4 decimals
  cat(paste(round(word_embeddings[target_word, 1:5], 4),
          collapse = " "), "\n")
} else {
  cat("The word '", target_word,
      "' was not found in the word embeddings.\n", sep = "")
  # Optionally show a few available words
  cat("Here are a few available words:\n")
  print(head(rownames(word_embeddings), 5))
}
```

Output

```
## First 10 values of word vector for 'machine':
## -0.2321 0.4529 -0.1757 -0.2689 0.3457
```

Each number contributes to the meaning of the word in the embedding space. Words that are used in similar ways will have vectors with similar numeric values.

Step 9: Find Similar Words Using Cosine Similarity

We can find words that mean something like "machine" by using something called cosine similarity. This method compares the word's number lists to see which ones point in a similar direction. It then gives us the ten words that are closest in meaning based on how they show up in the text.

R Code

```
# Compute cosine similarities
cos_sim <- sim2(
  x = word_embeddings,
  y = word_embeddings["machine", , drop = FALSE],
  method = "cosine",
  norm = "l2"
)


# Extract top 10 most similar words to "machine"
top_similar <- head(sort(cos_sim[, 1], decreasing = TRUE), 10)


# Nicely formatted vertical output
cat("Top 10 most similar words to 'machine':\n")
```

Output

```
## Top 10 most similar words to 'machine':
```

R Code

```
for (i in seq_along(top_similar)) {
  cat(sprintf(
    "%2d. %-15s %.4f\n", i,
    names(top_similar)[i], top_similar[i]
  ))
}
```

Output

```
##  1. machine         1.0000
##  2. text            0.1742
##  3. for             0.0859
##  4. learning        0.0855
##  5. popular         0.0782
##  6. bert            0.0438
##  7. love            0.0094
##  8. such            0.0039
##  9. word           -0.0281
## 10. and            -0.0461
```

The word "machine" will have a similarity score of 1 since it's being compared to itself. Other words, such as "learning" or "models," may appear with high scores if they often appear in similar contexts.

Step 10: Understand Contextual Embeddings

Traditional word embeddings like GloVe give each word just one fixed set of numbers, no matter where the word appears. So, a word like "bank" gets the same numbers whether it means a place to keep money or the side of a river.

But many words have different meanings depending on the sentence. Contextual embeddings fix this by creating different number sets for the same word based on the words around it. For example, if the sentence is about taking money out, "bank" gets a number set that means the money place. If it's about a river, it gets a number set for the river side. Models like ELMo and BERT use deep learning to make these smarter, context-based embeddings, helping computers understand language more like people do. You usually don't run these models in R, but it's good to know about them because they're key to most modern language tools.

Wrap-Up

In this lab, we learned how word embeddings help capture the meaning of words based on how they are used in text. We started with a small collection of sentences, made a table showing how often words appear near each other, and then trained a GloVe model to turn words into sets of numbers. These number sets reflect how words relate to one another, letting us find similar words and understand connections. We also talked about a drawback of older methods that give the same number set to a word no matter where it appears. To fix this, we introduced contextual embeddings, which create different number sets for a word depending on the sentence it's in. These newer approaches are the backbone of today's language technologies, helping computers grasp subtle meanings and analyze text more accurately.

Exercises

Word and Contextual Embeddings

Word embeddings convert words into numeric vectors that capture semantic meaning based on context. This exercise will work with small datasets to practice building embeddings and interpreting similarity results.

Dataset 1: Short sentences about technology topics

```
R Code
tech_texts <- c(
  "AI and machine learning are transforming industries.",
  "Data science uses statistics  to extract insights.",
  "Cloud computing and big data enable scalable solutions."
)
```

1. Break the `tech_texts` dataset into individual words, turn all words into lowercase, and use `itoken()` to create an iterator over the words.
2. From this iterator, build a list of all unique words, then remove any words that appear less than once. How many unique words remain?
3. Using a skip-gram window size of 3, make a term co-occurrence matrix (TCM) that counts how often words appear near each other. What size is this matrix?
4. Train a GloVe model on the TCM with 20 number values per word and run it for 15 rounds.
5. Find and display the list of numbers representing the word `"data"`.

Dataset 2: Short sentences about animals and nature

```
R Code
nature_texts <- c(
  "Lions and tigers are big cats found in the wild.",
  "Birds like eagles and hawks have excellent vision.",
  "Marine animals such as whales and dolphins live in oceans."
)
```

6. Break the `nature_texts` dataset into single words, change all words to lowercase, and make an iterator to go through them.
7. Build a vocabulary from these words and remove any that appear less than once. How many unique words are left?
8. Create a term co-occurrence matrix (TCM) using a window size of 4 to count how often words appear near each other. What are the dimensions of this matrix?
9. Train a GloVe model on this matrix using 30 numbers per word and run it for 20 cycles.
10. Using the embeddings, find the 5 words that are most similar to `"whales"` based on cosine similarity and list them.

Dataset 3: Short sentences about cooking and food

```
R Code
food_texts <- c(
  "Baking bread requires flour, water, and yeast.",
  "Spices like cinnamon and nutmeg add flavor to dishes.",
  "Grilling meats and vegetables gives a smoky taste."
)
```

11. Split the `food_texts` dataset into individual words and make an itera-tor to process them.

12. From these words, build a vocabulary and remove any word that ap-pears fewer than once. How many words are in the final vocabulary?

13. Use a window size of 2 to create a term co-occurrence matrix (TCM) that counts how often words appear near each other. Take a look at a 4 by 4 section of this matrix.

14. Train a GloVe model on this matrix with vectors of length 25, running the training for 10 rounds.

15. Get the embedding vector for the word `"flour"` and explain what these numbers mean in terms of representing the word.

Lab 8

Rule-Based Sentiment Analysis

Rule-based sentiment analysis relies on preset lists of words to figure out the mood of a piece of text. In this lab, you'll learn how to analyze customer reviews using sentiment dictionaries like AFINN and Bing. You'll break the reviews into words, match them with sentiment scores from the dictionaries, and then decide if each review is positive or negative based on those scores. This method is common in natural language processing for understanding feelings in things like product reviews, tweets, and surveys.

Lesson Steps

Step 1: Install and Load Required Libraries

Before starting, you need to install and load the packages used.

```
R Code
# Install if not already installed
options(repos = c(CRAN = "https://cran.r-project.org"))
install.packages(c("tidytext", "dplyr", "ggplot2",
                   "readr", "textdata"))

library(tidytext)
library(dplyr)
library(ggplot2)
library(readr)
library(textdata)
```

Step 2: Create the Review Dataset

The dataset contains 15 bakery reviews along with manually assigned sentiments.

R Code

```
reviews_df <- data.frame(
  review_text = c(
    "The bread was fresh and delicious.",
    "The service was slow and rude.",
    "Not bad but not great",
    "Absolutely loved the cupcakes!",
    "The coffee was terrible.",
    "Friendly staff and cozy atmosphere.",
    "Stale muffins and overpriced drinks.",
    "I didn't like the croissant.",
    "The cake was not bad.",
    "The tea was okay",
    "Delicious food but very slow service.",
    "Awful customer service ruined it.",
    "Best bakery in town!",
    "Not the worst place I have been to.",
    "The scones were dry"
  ),
  original_sentiment = c(
    "Positive", "Negative", "Neutral", "Positive", "Negative",
    "Positive", "Negative", "Negative", "Positive", "Neutral",
    "Mixed", "Negative", "Positive", "Neutral", "Mixed"
  ),
  stringsAsFactors = FALSE
)

print(reviews_df)
```

```
Output
##                                  review_text original_sentiment
## 1        The bread was fresh and delicious.            Positive
## 2            The service was slow and rude.            Negative
## 3                   Not bad but not great             Neutral
## 4            Absolutely loved the cupcakes!            Positive
## 5                   The coffee was terrible.            Negative
## 6       Friendly staff and cozy atmosphere.            Positive
## 7      Stale muffins and overpriced drinks.            Negative
## 8                I didn't like the croissant.            Negative
## 9                     The cake was not bad.             Positive
## 10                     The tea was okay              Neutral
## 11 Delicious food but very slow service.               Mixed
## 12       Awful customer service ruined it.             Negative
## 13                    Best bakery in town!              Positive
## 14   Not the worst place I have been to.              Neutral
## 15                   The scones were dry                Mixed
```

Step 3: Tokenize the Reviews

Tokenization splits each review into individual words. This allows us to compare each word individually to the entries in a sentiment lexicon.

R Code

```
reviews_df <- mutate(reviews_df, review_id = row_number())
tokenized_reviews <- unnest_tokens(reviews_df, word,
                                   review_text)


# Show the first 10 tokenized words with their review IDs
print("Sample of tokenized reviews:")
```

Output

```
## [1] "Sample of tokenized reviews:"
```

R Code

```
print(head(tokenized_reviews, 10))
```

Output

```
##    original_sentiment review_id      word
## 1            Positive         1       the
## 2            Positive         1     bread
## 3            Positive         1       was
## 4            Positive         1     fresh
## 5            Positive         1       and
## 6            Positive         1 delicious
## 7            Negative         2       the
## 8            Negative         2   service
## 9            Negative         2       was
## 10           Negative         2      slow
```

Step 4: Apply the AFINN Lexicon

The AFINN lexicon gives each word a sentiment score ranging from -5 to +5. First, we match our list of words with these scores, then add up the scores for all the words in each review.

R Code
```
afinn <- get_sentiments("afinn")


joined_reviews <- merge(tokenized_reviews, afinn, by = "word")


print("Sample of tokenized words joined with AFINN scores:")
```

Output
```
## [1] "Sample of tokenized words joined with AFINN scores:"
```

R Code
```
print(head(joined_reviews, 10))
```

Output

```
##          word original_sentiment review_id value
## 1       awful           Negative        12    -3
## 2         bad           Positive         9    -3
## 3         bad            Neutral         3    -3
## 4        best           Positive        13     3
## 5       fresh           Positive         1     1
## 6    friendly           Positive         6     2
## 7       great            Neutral         3     3
## 8        like           Negative         8     2
## 9       loved           Positive         4     3
## 10     ruined           Negative        12    -2
```

R Code

```r
# Summarize sentiment scores by review_id
review_sentiment <- aggregate(value ~ review_id,
                              data = joined_reviews, sum)

print("Sentiment score summary for each review:")
```

Output

```
## [1] "Sentiment score summary for each review:"
```

R Code

```r
print(review_sentiment)
```

Output

```
##    review_id value
## 1          1     1
## 2          3     0
## 3          4     3
## 4          5    -3
## 5          6     2
## 6          8     2
## 7          9    -3
## 8         12    -5
## 9         13     3
## 10        14    -3
```

R Code

```r
scored_reviews <- summarise(
  group_by(joined_reviews, review_id),
  total_score = sum(value),
  .groups = "drop"
)

scored_reviews <- mutate(
  scored_reviews,
  predicted_sentiment = case_when(
    total_score > 0 ~ "Positive",
    total_score < 0 ~ "Negative",
    TRUE ~ "Neutral"
  )
)

print(scored_reviews)
```

Output

```
## # A tibble: 10 x 3
##    review_id total_score predicted_sentiment
##        <int>       <dbl> <chr>
## 1          1           1 Positive
## 2          3           0 Neutral
## 3          4           3 Positive
## 4          5          -3 Negative
## 5          6           2 Positive
## 6          8           2 Positive
## 7          9          -3 Negative
## 8         12          -5 Negative
## 9         13           3 Positive
## 10        14          -3 Negative
```

Step 5: Visualize AFINN Sentiment Results

We can visualize the predicted sentiment distribution based on AFINN scores using a bar plot.

R Code

```r
ggplot(scored_reviews, aes(x = predicted_sentiment)) +
  geom_bar(fill = "#637D8D") +
  labs(
    title = "Bakery Review Sentiment (AFINN)",
    x = "Predicted Sentiment",
    y = "Number of Reviews"
  ) +
  theme_minimal()
```

Bakery Review Sentiment (AFINN)

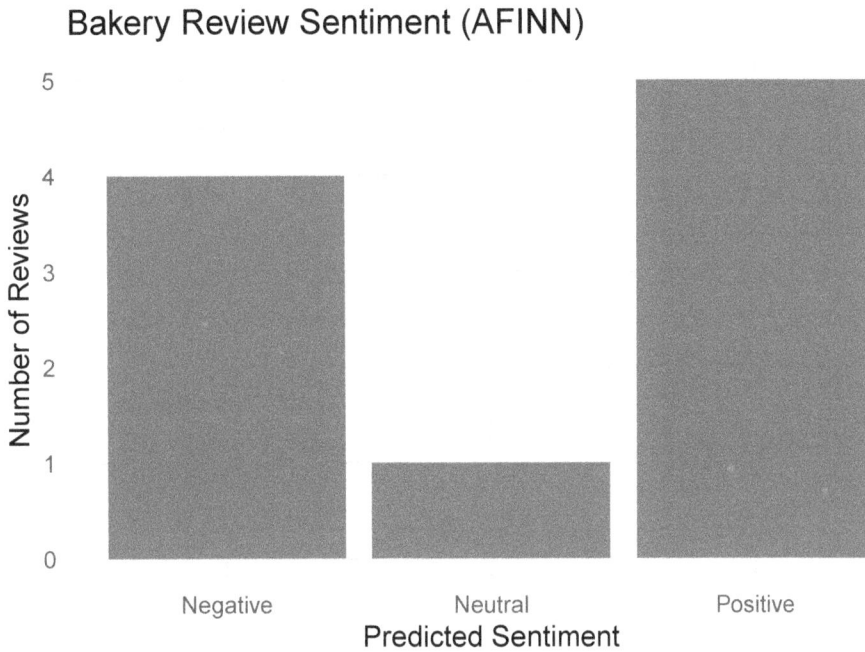

Step 6: Apply the Bing Lexicon

Let's look at another popular lexicon. The Bing lexicon doesn't use numbers—it simply marks each word as either "positive" or "negative." Let's use it by first loading the lexicon. Next tokenize or break the reviews into individual words again.

R Code

```
# Load Bing sentiment lexicon
bing <- get_sentiments("bing")


# Tokenize reviews and convert to lowercase
# (default behavior of unnest_tokens)
reviews_df$review_id <- seq_len(nrow(reviews_df))
tokenized_reviews <- unnest_tokens(reviews_df,
  word, review_text,
  to_lower = TRUE
)


# Join tokens with Bing sentiment labels
bing_joined <- inner_join(tokenized_reviews,
  bing,
  by = "word"
)


# View matched sentiment words
head(bing_joined)
```

Output

```
##   original_sentiment review_id      word sentiment
## 1           Positive         1     fresh  positive
## 2           Positive         1 delicious  positive
## 3           Negative         2      slow  negative
## 4           Negative         2      rude  negative
## 5            Neutral         3       bad  negative
## 6            Neutral         3     great  positive
```

Step 7: Count and Score Bing Sentiment

We count how many positive and negative words appear in each review. Then we reshape the data to a wide format and find the overall score by subtracting the number of negative words from the number of positive ones.

```
R Code
# Count the number of positive and negative words
bing_counts <- count(bing_joined, review_id, sentiment)


# Convert to wide format for scoring
bing_wide <- tidyr::pivot_wider(
  data = bing_counts,
  names_from = sentiment,
  values_from = n,
  values_fill = list(n = 0)
)


# Ensure both sentiment columns exist
if (!"positive" %in% colnames(bing_wide)) {
  bing_wide$positive <- 0
}
if (!"negative" %in% colnames(bing_wide)) {
  bing_wide$negative <- 0
}


# Calculate sentiment score
bing_wide$score <- bing_wide$positive - bing_wide$negative


# Assign predicted sentiment label
bing_wide$predicted_sentiment <- ifelse(
  bing_wide$score > 0, "Positive",
```

```
    ifelse(bing_wide$score < 0, "Negative", "Neutral")
)
```

Step 8: Merge Bing Results with Original Reviews

Next merge the review data with the Bing results to compare predicted sentiment to original labels (which were hand made).

```
R Code
reviews_with_bing_sentiment <- merge(
  reviews_df,
  bing_wide[, c("review_id", "score",
                "predicted_sentiment")],
  by = "review_id",
  all.x = TRUE
)

print(reviews_with_bing_sentiment[,1:2])
```

Output

```
##    review_id                          review_text
## 1          1     The bread was fresh and delicious.
## 2          2        The service was slow and rude.
## 3          3                Not bad but not great
## 4          4            Absolutely loved the cupcakes!
## 5          5                The coffee was terrible.
## 6          6     Friendly staff and cozy atmosphere.
## 7          7     Stale muffins and overpriced drinks.
## 8          8            I didn't like the croissant.
## 9          9                 The cake was not bad.
## 10        10                    The tea was okay
## 11        11 Delicious food but very slow service.
## 12        12     Awful customer service ruined it.
## 13        13                 Best bakery in town!
## 14        14     Not the worst place I have been to.
## 15        15               The scones were dry
```

R Code

```
print(reviews_with_bing_sentiment[,3:5])
```

Output

```
##     original_sentiment score predicted_sentiment
## 1               Positive     2             Positive
## 2               Negative    -2             Negative
## 3                Neutral     0              Neutral
## 4               Positive     1             Positive
## 5               Negative    -1             Negative
## 6               Positive     2             Positive
## 7               Negative    -2             Negative
## 8               Negative     1             Positive
## 9               Positive    -1             Negative
## 10               Neutral    NA                 <NA>
## 11                 Mixed     0              Neutral
## 12              Negative    -2             Negative
## 13              Positive     1             Positive
## 14               Neutral    -1             Negative
## 15                 Mixed    NA                 <NA>
```

Step 9: Visualize Bing Sentiment Results

Let's make a bar chart to show visually how reviews were classified using the
Bing lexicon.

R Code

```
ggplot(reviews_with_bing_sentiment,
  aes(x = predicted_sentiment)) +
  geom_bar(fill = "#EE6C4D") +
  labs(
    title = "Bakery Review Sentiment (Bing)",
    x = "Predicted Sentiment",
    y = "Number of Reviews"
  ) +
  theme_minimal()
```

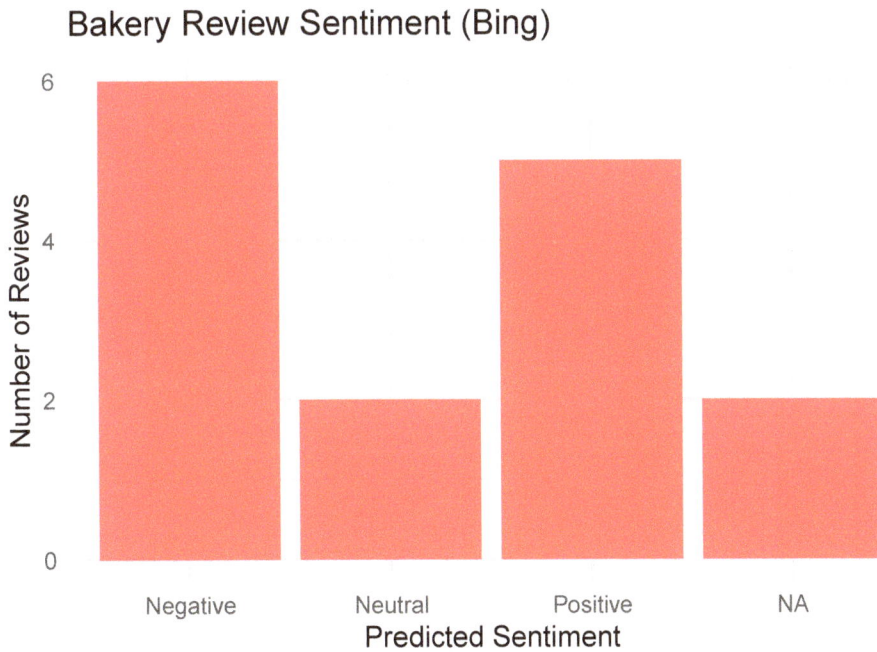

Bakery Review Sentiment (Bing)

Wrap-Up

In this lab, you practiced doing rule-based sentiment analysis using two well-known word lists: AFINN and Bing. You broke down review text into words, matched them with the lexicons, figured out the overall sentiment, and visualized what you found. AFINN helped you measure how strong the emotion was, while Bing made it easy to tell if a word was positive or negative. These simple but powerful methods are often used in real-world projects and are a great starting point for working with text data.

Exercises

Rule-Based Sentiment Analysis

Rule-based sentiment analysis uses predefined lexicons to determine the emotional tone or 'sentiment' of text data. This exercise gives you practice in rule based sentiment analysis.

Dataset 1: Bakery Customer Reviews

```
R Code
reviews_df <- data.frame(
  review_text = c(
    "The bread was fresh and delicious.",
    "The service was slow and rude.",
    "Not bad but not great",
    "Absolutely loved the cupcakes!",
    "The coffee was terrible.",
    "Friendly staff and cozy atmosphere.",
    "Stale muffins and overpriced drinks.",
    "I didn't like the croissant.",
    "The cake was not bad.",
    "The tea was okay",
    "Delicious food but very slow service.",
    "Awful customer service ruined it.",
    "Best bakery in town!",
    "Not the worst place I have been to.",
    "The scones were dry"
  ),
  stringsAsFactors = FALSE
)
```

1. Start by breaking each review into separate words and changing all the words to lowercase so everything is consistent.
2. Then, match these words with their sentiment values from the AFINN word list.
3. For each review, add up the scores of all its words to get a total sentiment score.
4. Use that total to label the review: call it Positive if the score is above zero, Negative if it's below zero, and Neutral if the score is exactly zero.
5. Finally, make a bar chart that shows how many reviews fall into each category—Positive, Negative, or Neutral—for the bakery reviews.

Dataset 2: Movie Reviews

```
R Code
movie_reviews <- data.frame(
  review_text = c(
    "The plot was predictable but the acting was great.",
    "Absolutely loved the cinematography!",
    "Terrible movie, wasted two hours.",
    "The soundtrack was good but the story was dull.",
    "A masterpiece with brilliant performances.",
    "Not my type of film, but well made.",
    "Could have been better, some parts were boring.",
    "Enjoyed every minute of the movie.",
    "Poorly written script and bad directing.",
    "A fun and thrilling experience."
  ),
  stringsAsFactors = FALSE
)
```

6. Take the `movie_reviews` and split each review into separate words,

making sure all the words are lowercase.

7. Next, match each word with its sentiment from the Bing list, which marks words as either "positive" or "negative."

8. Go through each review and count how many positive and negative words it contains.

9. Figure out a sentiment score by subtracting the number of negative words from the number of positive ones.

10. Based on that score, label each review as Positive if the score is above zero, Negative if it's below zero, or Neutral if it's exactly zero.

Dataset 3: Restaurant Reviews

```
R Code
restaurant_reviews <- data.frame(
  review_text = c(
    "The waiter was very rude and slow.",
    "Delicious food and excellent service.",
    "The place was clean but the food was bland.",
    "I loved the dessert but hated the main course.",
    "Great atmosphere and friendly staff.",
    "Not worth the price.",
    "Will definitely come back again!",
    "Mediocre food and slow service.",
    "Best dining experience in years.",
    "Overcooked steak but tasty sides."
  ),
  stringsAsFactors = FALSE
)
```

11. Break each review in the `restaurant_reviews` dataset into individual words and make all the letters lowercase for consistency.

12. Match these words with their sentiment values using the AFINN list, which gives each word a score.
13. Add up the scores for all the words in each review to get a total sentiment value.
14. Based on that total, give each review a label: Positive if the number is above zero, Negative if it's below zero, or Neutral if it's exactly zero.
15. Finally, make a bar chart to show how many reviews fall into each of the three categories—Positive, Negative, or Neutral.

Lab 9

Machine Learning-Based Sentiment Analysis

Machine learning lets computers figure out how to do tasks by looking at lots of examples. For instance, if you want a computer to tell whether a movie review is positive or negative, you don't have to explain all the rules that make a review good or bad. Instead, you show the computer many reviews that are already labeled as "positive" or "negative."

The computer (the machine) looks for patterns in the words people use and learns how to guess the sentiment of new reviews. This learning process of providing existing data is called training the model. After that, the model can decide if new reviews not in the training data and provided no labels are positive or negative all by itself.

In this lab, you'll use a method called Naive Bayes to classify the sentiment of reviews based on examples.

Lesson Steps

Step 1: Setup

This code installs and loads the necessary packages.

```
R Code
# Install if not already installed
options(repos = c(CRAN = "https://cran.r-project.org"))
# Only run once
install.packages(c("text2vec", "caret", "e1071", "tm"))


# Load libraries
library(text2vec)
library(caret)
library(e1071)
library(tm)
```

Next create a sample dataset.

R Code

```
# Create example reviews and sentiment labels

text <- c(
  "I love this movie",
  "This film is terrible",
  "It was a great experience",
  "I hated every minute",
  "Absolutely fantastic!",
  "Not good at all",
  "Really enjoyable",
  "It was boring"
)

sentiment <- as.factor(c(
  "positive", "negative", "positive", "negative",
  "positive", "negative", "positive", "negative"
))

data <- data.frame(
  text = text, sentiment = sentiment,
  stringsAsFactors = FALSE
)
```

Step 2: Clean the text

This function prepares the text by converting it to lowercase, removing punctuation and stopwords, and trimming extra spaces.

R Code
```r
clean_text <- function(x) {
  x <- tolower(x)
  x <- removePunctuation(x)
  x <- removeWords(x, stopwords("en"))
  x <- stripWhitespace(x)
  return(x)
}


data$text_clean <- sapply(data$text, clean_text)


# View the first 2 cleaned text entries
cat("Sample cleaned text:\n")
```

Output
```
## Sample cleaned text:
```

R Code
```r
print(head(data$text_clean, 2))
```

Output
```
## [1] " love movie"    " film terrible"
```

Step 3: Convert text to TF-IDF

This code turns text into a numeric format using TF-IDF, which measures how important a word is in a document compared to all others. (Learning this was covered in an earlier lab.)

R Code
```
it <- itoken(data$text_clean, progressbar = FALSE)
vocab <- create_vocabulary(it)

# Show the first 10 vocabulary terms with their counts
cat("Vocabulary sample:\n")
```

Output
```
## Vocabulary sample:
```

R Code
```
print(head(vocab, 10))
```

Output

```
## Number of docs: 8
## 0 stopwords:  ...
## ngram_min = 1; ngram_max = 1
## Vocabulary:
##            term term_count doc_count
##          <char>     <int>     <int>
##  1: absolutely         1         1
##  2:     boring         1         1
##  3:   enjoyable         1         1
##  4:       every         1         1
##  5: experience         1         1
##  6:   fantastic         1         1
##  7:        film         1         1
##  8:        good         1         1
##  9:       great         1         1
## 10:       hated         1         1
```

R Code

```
vectorizer <- vocab_vectorizer(vocab)
dtm <- create_dtm(it, vectorizer)


tfidf <- TfIdf$new()
dtm_tfidf <- fit_transform(dtm, tfidf)


# Check dimensions of the TF-IDF matrix
cat("TF-IDF matrix dimensions:", dim(dtm_tfidf), "\n")
```

Output
```
## TF-IDF matrix dimensions: 8 15
```

Step 4: Split data into train and test sets

We split the dataset into a training set (used to teach the model) and a test set (used to see how well it performs). A test set of known values is used (vs completely new unlabeled data) which is simply a random split from the original data. Here we will do a 75% partition of the data for training the residual 25% for testing.

R Code
```
set.seed(42)

train_index <- createDataPartition(data$sentiment,
                    p = 0.75, list = FALSE)

train_data <- dtm_tfidf[train_index, ]
test_data <- dtm_tfidf[-train_index, ]

train_labels <- data$sentiment[train_index]
test_labels <- data$sentiment[-train_index]

cat("Training set size:", length(train_labels), "\n")
```

Output
```
## Training set size: 6
```

R Code
```
cat("Test set size:", length(test_labels), "\n")
```

Output
```
## Test set size: 2
```

Step 5: Train and test a Naive Bayes model

This code will apply the Naive Bayes model using the training data and predicts sentiment on the test data.

R Code
```
model_nb <- naiveBayes(as.matrix(train_data), train_labels)
predictions <- predict(model_nb, as.matrix(test_data))
```

A confusion matrix shows how many test examples were correctly or incorrectly classified. You can interpret the model's performance by comparing the predicted versus actual labels. Accuracy is the percent correctly classified.

R Code
```
conf_mat <- confusionMatrix(predictions, test_labels)

print(conf_mat)
```

Output

```
## Confusion Matrix and Statistics
##
##           Reference
## Prediction negative positive
##    negative      1        1
##    positive      0        0
##
##              Accuracy : 0.5
##                95% CI : (0.0126, 0.9874)
##    No Information Rate : 0.5
##    P-Value [Acc > NIR] : 0.75
##
##                 Kappa : 0
##
##  Mcnemar's Test P-Value : 1.00
##
##             Sensitivity : 1.0
##             Specificity : 0.0
##          Pos Pred Value : 0.5
##          Neg Pred Value : NaN
##              Prevalence : 0.5
##          Detection Rate : 0.5
##    Detection Prevalence : 1.0
##       Balanced Accuracy : 0.5
##
##        'Positive' Class : negative
##
```

Wrap-Up

In this lab, you applied the Naive Bayes method to classify movie reviews as either positive or negative. You started by cleaning and preparing the text, then turned the words into numbers using TF-IDF. After splitting the data into training and test groups, you trained the model and checked how well it performed. This showed how even a simple machine learning approach can learn from examples and accurately predict sentiment in new reviews.

Exercises

Machine Learning-Based Sentiment Analysis

Machine learning enables computers to learn from examples rather than explicit programming. These exercises practice the use of Naive Bayes to classify text sentiment by training on labeled reviews and testing accuracy.

Dataset 1: Movie Reviews (Binary Sentiment)

```
R Code
movie_reviews <- data.frame(
  text = c(
    "I love this movie",
    "This film is terrible",
    "It was a great experience",
    "I hated every minute",
    "Absolutely fantastic!",
    "Not good at all",
    "Really enjoyable",
    "It was boring"
  ),
  sentiment = as.factor(c(
    "positive", "negative", "positive", "negative",
    "positive", "negative", "positive", "negative"
  )),
  stringsAsFactors = FALSE
)
```

1. Start by cleaning the `movie_reviews` text: make everything lowercase, get rid of punctuation, remove common words that don't add meaning

(stopwords), and trim any extra spaces.

2. Build a list of all the words used (vocabulary) and turn the cleaned text into a Document-Term Matrix using TF-IDF to weigh the importance of each word.

3. Divide the data so that 75% is for training the model and 25% for testing it, making sure the split keeps the same balance of positive and negative reviews.

4. Use the training data to teach a Naive Bayes model how to recognize sentiment based on the TF-IDF features and their labels.

5. Finally, use the model to predict sentiment on the test data and create a confusion matrix to see how well the predictions match the actual labels.

Dataset 2: Product Reviews (Binary Sentiment)

R Code

```
product_reviews <- data.frame(
  text = c(
    "The product is excellent and works well.",
    "Completely useless, stopped working after a day.",
    "I am very satisfied with my purchase.",
    "Worst product ever, do not buy.",
    "Highly recommend this to everyone.",
    "Not worth the money.",
    "Good quality and fast shipping.",
    "Terrible experience, very disappointed."
  ),
  sentiment = as.factor(c(
    "positive", "negative", "positive", "negative",
    "positive", "negative", "positive", "negative"
  )),
  stringsAsFactors = FALSE
)
```

6. Clean the text in `product_reviews` the same way you did before—lowercase everything, remove punctuation and common filler words, and trim spaces.

7. Create a Document-Term Matrix weighted by TF-IDF from the cleaned product reviews.

8. Split the dataset so that 75% is used to train the model and 25% is kept aside for testing, making sure the groups have the same balance of classes.

9. Train a Naive Bayes classifier using the training data.

10. Test the model on the test set, then check how accurate it is and look at the confusion matrix to see how well it did.

Dataset 3: Restaurant Reviews (Binary Sentiment)

```
R Code
restaurant_reviews <- data.frame(
  text = c(
    "Loved the food and the service was great!",
    "The meal was cold and bland.",
    "Amazing atmosphere and friendly staff.",
    "I will never come back here again.",
    "Best dining experience I've had.",
    "Disappointing, the waiter was rude.",
    "Fantastic desserts and cocktails.",
    "Food was mediocre and overpriced."
  ),
  sentiment = as.factor(c(
    "positive", "negative", "positive", "negative",
    "positive", "negative", "positive", "negative"
  )),
  stringsAsFactors = FALSE
)
```

11. Clean the `restaurant_reviews` text the same way as you did with the earlier datasets—convert to lowercase, remove punctuation and stop-words, and trim spaces.

12. Use the cleaned text to build a Document-Term Matrix weighted by TF-IDF.

13. Divide the data into training and test sets, with 75% for training and 25% for testing, making sure to keep the sentiment balance consistent.

14. Train a Naive Bayes model using the training data, then use it to predict sentiment on the test set.

15. Create a confusion matrix from the test predictions and explain what

it tells you about the model's performance.

Lab 10

Named Entity Recognition (NER)

Named Entity Recognition, or NER, is basically teaching computers how to spot important names or places in text—things like people, cities, or companies. When you read a news story, you naturally pick up on names and places, but computers need some guidance to do the same. NER helps the computer automatically find these key words so it can make sense of the text better. For example, in "Barack Obama was born in Hawaii," NER lets the computer recognize that "Barack Obama" is a person and "Hawaii" is a location. This kind of tool is really useful when you're dealing with lots of text, like news articles or social media. In this lab, you'll get hands-on experience using R and a package called UDPipe to find these named entities in sentences.

Lesson Steps

Step 1: Install and Load Required Packages

To start, we need to install and load the `udpipe` package. This package provides tools for linguistic annotation using pre-trained models.

```
R Code
# Install if not already installed
options(repos = c(CRAN = "https://cran.r-project.org"))
# Only run once
install.packages("udpipe")


library(udpipe)
```

Step 2: Download and Load a Pre-Trained English Model

NER requires a language model that understands English grammar and syntax. We download a pre-trained English model that contains the data needed to perform linguistic analysis.

Run the following code to download the model. This only needs to be done once:

```
R Code
model <- udpipe_download_model(language = "english")
```

Once downloaded, load the model into R with this command:

```
R Code
ud_model <- udpipe_load_model(file = model$file_model)
```

Now, the ud_model object contains the loaded model ready for analyzing text.

Step 3: Prepare Example Text for Analysis

Now, put together a list of sample sentences that mention things like people's names, company names, and places. You'll use these sentences as
input for the named entity recognition tool.

```
R Code
text <- c(
   "Barack Obama was born in Hawaii.",
   "Google is a tech company based in California.",
   "The Eiffel Tower is in Paris."
)
```

This vector stores multiple sentences as one object, making it easier to process them.

Step 4: Annotate the Text Using the Model

Next, we run the udpipe_annotate() function to process our text. This function uses the model we loaded along with the list of sentences you created.
It breaks each sentence down into individual pieces like words and punctuation marks, then adds information about each piece—such as its base
form (lemma), its part of speech, and how it relates to other words in the
sentence.

Because the raw output is detailed and a bit hard to read, we turn it into a
data frame so it's easier to look at and work with.

```
R Code
annotation <- udpipe_annotate(ud_model, x = text)
annotated_df <- as.data.frame(annotation)
```

You can use the look at selected features in the annotation table:

R Code

```
head(annotated_df[,4:5])
```

Output

```
##                        sentence token_id
## 1 Barack Obama was born in Hawaii.        1
## 2 Barack Obama was born in Hawaii.        2
## 3 Barack Obama was born in Hawaii.        3
## 4 Barack Obama was born in Hawaii.        4
## 5 Barack Obama was born in Hawaii.        5
## 6 Barack Obama was born in Hawaii.        6
```

R Code

```
head(annotated_df[,5:7])
```

Output

```
##   token_id  token  lemma
## 1        1 Barack Barack
## 2        2  Obama  Obama
## 3        3    was     be
## 4        4   born   bear
## 5        5     in     in
## 6        6 Hawaii Hawaii
```

Step 5: Extract Named Entities from the Annotation

To identify named entities, filter the annotated data frame for tokens classified as proper nouns. Proper nouns usually represent names of people, places, or organizations.

We subset the data frame where the part of speech tag (upos) equals "PROPN":

R Code
```
named_entities <- subset(annotated_df, upos == "PROPN")
```

Then, to see the results print the tokens and lemmas:

R Code
```
print(named_entities[, c("token", "lemma")])
```

Output
```
##              token        lemma
## 1          Barack       Barack
## 2           Obama        Obama
## 6          Hawaii       Hawaii
## 8          Google       Google
## 15     California   California
## 18         Eiffel       Eiffel
## 19          Tower        Tower
## 22          Paris        Paris
```

This shows the named entities found in the text, along with their base forms and which sentence they came from.

Wrap Up

In this lab, you learned how to use the udpipe package in R for Named Entity Recognition. After downloading and loading a ready-made model, you annotated some sample text to pull out important entities. Named Entity Recognition is a key technique in many language-related tasks.

Exercises

Named Entity Recognition (NER)

In this exercise, you will use the `udpipe` package in R to perform NER on different example datasets.

Dataset 1: News Headlines about Technology

```
R Code
text1 <- c(
  "Apple released the new iPhone in California.",
  "Elon Musk announced SpaceX's Mars mission.",
  "Microsoft acquires AI startup OpenAI."
)
```

1. Start by loading the `udpipe` package and, if you haven't already, download the English language model.
2. Use the UDPipe model to analyze the sentences stored in `text1`, then convert the output into a data frame for easier handling.
3. Take a look at the first 10 rows of this annotated data to get a feel for the results.
4. Find and list all the proper nouns—words tagged as `PROPN`—including their original form, base form (lemma), and which sentence they came from.
5. Finally, check the first sentence to see which named entities like people, companies, or places show up there.

Dataset 2: Sentences about Historical Events

```
R Code
text2 <- c(
  "Neil Armstrong landed on the Moon in 1969.",
  "The Berlin Wall fell in Germany in 1989.",
  "The Declaration of Independence was signed in Philadelphia."
)
```

6. Analyze the sentences in `text2` using the UDPipe model and turn the results into a data frame.
7. Pull out all the proper nouns from this data and display them just like before.
8. Make a list of all the places mentioned in the sentences, focusing on location names.
9. Find any dates or years included in the text by checking the part-of-speech tags or looking for numbers.
10. Discuss why it's useful to recognize dates along with proper nouns when analyzing text.

Dataset 3: Social Media Posts

```
R Code
text3 <- c(
  "Had a great time visiting the Statue of Liberty in NYC!",
  "Congrats to @NASA on the successful Mars rover landing!",
  "Amazon is expanding its headquarters in Seattle."
)
```

11. Use the UDPipe model to annotate `text3` and convert the results into

a data frame.

12. From that data, pull out and show the named entities, paying special attention to organizations and places.

13. Look for any entities that might be overlooked because they include special characters like "@," which are common in social media posts.

14. Suggest one tool or method that can help improve named entity recognition when working with social media text.

15. Explain why recognizing entities in social media writing can be harder than doing the same in formal news articles.

Lab 11

Latent Dirichlet Allocation (LDA)

Introduction

Latent Dirichlet Allocation, or LDA for short, is a method used to find hidden topics in collections of text—like articles, blog posts, or social media updates. Think of it like going through a pile of magazines and figuring out what they're mostly about, whether it's sports, science, or fashion, without having to read every word. LDA does this by looking at how words show up together across different texts. It finds patterns and groups of words that often appear in the same context, then uses that to guess what topics are being discussed. One key thing about LDA is that it doesn't expect each piece of writing to stick to just one topic. It can tell when a single article mixes several themes, and it estimates how much of each topic shows up in that piece. In this lab, you'll use R to try out LDA on a small group of sample sentences and see how it works in practice.

Lesson Steps

Step 1: Set Up

First, we install and load a few R packages that help with cleaning and analyzing text. These include tm for text mining, topicmodels for running LDA, tidytext to work with the results in a tidy format, and dplyr for organizing and filtering the data.

```
R Code
# Install if not already installed
options(repos = c(CRAN = "https://cran.r-project.org"))
# Install required packages (run once if needed)
install.packages(c("tm", "topicmodels", "tidytext", "dplyr"))


# Load libraries
library(tm)
library(topicmodels)
library(tidytext)
library(dplyr)
```

Let's put together a small set of six short text examples. Each one is just a sentence, and they're written about two general subjects—football and space. This gives us a simple dataset with two clear themes to explore using topic modeling

```
R Code
# Create a sample dataset
documents <- c(
"I love playing football with my friends on the weekend.",
"Space exploration and planets are interesting to me.",
"The new football season is starting soon, I can't wait!",
"Astronauts train for years to go on space missions.",
"My favorite player scored a goal in the football match.",
"NASA launched a new satellite to study stars and planets."
)
```

Step 2: Create and Clean the Text Corpus

Next, we turn the set of text into a corpus using the VCorpus function. A corpus is just a collection of text that's organized in a way that makes it easier to work with. It's kind of like the data table format key structure for structured data but the document key structure for unstructured text analytics instead.

After creating the corpus, we clean up or 'preprocess' the text to get it ready for analysis. That means changing everything to lowercase, getting rid of punctuation and numbers, removing common words like "the" and "and," and clearing out any extra spaces. Cleaning the text like this helps focus on the words that actually matter and gets rid of the fluff.

R Code
```
# Create corpus
corpus <- VCorpus(VectorSource(documents))

# Clean the text
corpus <- tm_map(corpus, content_transformer(tolower))
corpus <- tm_map(corpus, removePunctuation)
corpus <- tm_map(corpus, removeNumbers)
corpus <- tm_map(corpus, removeWords,
                 stopwords("english"))
corpus <- tm_map(corpus, stripWhitespace)



# Show cleaned text content for first 3 documents
content(corpus[[1]])
```

Output
```
## [1] " love playing football friends weekend"
```

R Code
```
content(corpus[[2]])
```

Output
```
## [1] "space exploration planets interesting "
```

R Code
```
content(corpus[[3]])
```

Output
```
## [1] " new football season starting soon cant wait"
```

Step 3: Create Document-Term Matrix

Once the text is cleaned, we turn it into a Document-Term Matrix. This is just a table that shows how often each word shows up in each document. Each row is a document, and each column is a word. The numbers tell you how many times that word appears in that document. After building the matrix, we check for any rows that are completely empty—this can happen if a sentence only had common words we filtered out. We get rid of those empty rows so everything runs smoothly when we apply the LDA model.

R Code
```
# Create DTM
dtm <- DocumentTermMatrix(corpus)

# Show DTM as matrix for first 3 documents and terms
dtm_matrix <- as.matrix(dtm)
dtm_matrix[1:3, 1:6]
```

Output
```
##        Terms
## Docs astronauts cant exploration favorite football friends
##    1           0    0           0        0        1       1
##    2           0    0           1        0        0       0
##    3           0    1           0        0        1       0
```

R Code
```
# Remove empty rows
dtm_matrix <- as.matrix(dtm)
non_empty_rows <- rowSums(dtm_matrix) > 0
dtm <- dtm[non_empty_rows, ]
```

Step 4: Apply LDA with Two Topics

Now that the document-term matrix is ready, we run the LDA model. Since our six text samples are about football and space, we tell the model to look for two topics. It goes through the word patterns in the documents and sorts the words into groups that it thinks belong together. We also set a random seed with control = list(seed = 1234) so we get the same results if we run the code again later.

R Code
```
# Apply LDA
lda_model <- LDA(dtm, k = 2,
               control = list(seed = 1234))


# Show summary of the model
lda_model
```

Output
```
## A LDA_VEM topic model with 2 topics.
```

Step 5: Extract Top Terms for Each Topic

After the model finishes running, we use the tidy function to organize the results in a way that's easier to work with. For each word, we get a beta value, which tells us how strongly that word is tied to a given topic. By looking at these values, we can start to figure out what each topic is mainly about based on the words that show up most often.

```
R Code
# Extract beta values
topics <- tidy(lda_model, matrix = "beta")


# Get top 6 terms per topic by beta
top_terms <- group_by(topics, topic)
top_terms <- slice_max(top_terms, beta, n = 6)
top_terms <- arrange(top_terms, topic, desc(beta))


top_terms
```

Output

```
## # A tibble: 12 x 3
## # Groups:    topic [2]
##    topic term      beta
##    <int> <chr>     <dbl>
## 1      1 planets  0.0800
## 2      1 football 0.0683
## 3      1 space    0.0585
## 4      1 new      0.0479
## 5      1 nasa     0.0439
## 6      1 friends  0.0430
## 7      2 football 0.108
## 8      2 new      0.0697
## 9      2 space    0.0592
## 10     2 soon     0.0558
## 11     2 missions 0.0435
## 12     2 match    0.0430
```

Now we can take a look at the results from the model. The output shows each topic alongside the words linked to it and their beta values. These values show how closely each word is connected to a topic—the higher the number, the stronger the connection. So if "exploration" has a beta of 0.0435 for topic 1 and only 0.0106 for topic 2, it's clearly more tied to topic 1. Some words, like "football," might show up in both topics but with different strengths, which just means they're relevant in more than one context. Looking at these numbers helps us understand what each topic is really about so we can give them clear, meaningful names.

Step 6: View the Top Five Terms per Topic

To make things easier to understand, we pull out the top five words for each topic—the ones with the highest beta values. These are the words that best represent what each topic is about. Looking at them helps us figure out the general theme of each group. For example, if a topic's top words include "football," "player," and "match," it's clearly about sports. If another topic shows words like "space," "astronauts," and "planets," then it's safe to say that one's about space.

```
R Code
# Get top 5 terms per topic
top_terms <- NULL
for (i in 1:2) {
  topic_i <- topics[topics$topic == i, ]
  top_i <- topic_i[order(-topic_i$beta), ][1:5, ]
  top_terms <- rbind(top_terms, top_i)
}

# Print top terms
print(top_terms)
```

```
Output
## # A tibble: 10 x 3
##    topic term        beta
##    <int> <chr>       <dbl>
## 1      1 planets    0.0800
## 2      1 football   0.0683
## 3      1 space      0.0585
## 4      1 new        0.0479
## 5      1 nasa       0.0439
## 6      2 football   0.108
## 7      2 new        0.0697
## 8      2 space      0.0592
## 9      2 soon       0.0558
## 10     2 missions   0.0435
```

This summary of the top five terms per topic gives us a quick, human-readable understanding of what the model found. These keywords allow us to label and interpret the abstract statistical results of LDA in a meaningful way.

Wrap-Up

In this lab, we used LDA to find hidden topics in a small set of short texts. We started by setting up the needed packages and creating a simple dataset. After cleaning the text and organizing it into a document-term matrix, we ran the LDA model to look for patterns. Once the model was done, we looked at the top words in each topic to figure out what they were about. Even with just a few sentences, the model picked up on the two main themes: football and space. On a bigger scale, this method can be really useful for sorting through large collections of text like articles, tweets, reviews, or research summaries.

Exercises

Latent Dirichlet Allocation (LDA)

In this exercise, you will apply LDA to small example datasets using R.

Dataset 1: Simple Sentences about Food and Travel

```
R Code
docs1 <- c(
  "I love trying new Italian restaurants in Rome.",
  "Pizza and pasta are my favorite Italian dishes.",
  "Exploring new countries broadens your horizons.",
  "Traveling allows me to taste authentic local food.",
  "The best way to learn about culture is through food."
)
```

1. Start by turning `docs1` into a text corpus. Then clean it up by making all the text lowercase, removing punctuation, numbers, common stop-words, and any extra spaces.
2. Use the cleaned text to create a Document-Term Matrix, and check its dimensions to see how many documents and unique words you've got.
3. Drop any rows that ended up empty—this can happen if a document didn't have any useful words left. After that, count how many documents are still in the dataset.
4. Run the LDA model on the matrix, asking it to find 2 topics. Set a random seed so your results are the same if you run it again later.
5. For each topic, pull out the top 5 words with the highest beta values—the ones that best represent what each topic is about—and print them.

Dataset 2: Sentences about Technology and Environment

R Code

```
docs2 <- c(
  "Solar energy is becoming a popular fuel alternative.",
  "New smartphone models have improved battery life.",
  "Climate change impacts weather patterns worldwide.",
  "Advancements in AI are reshaping industries.",
  "Renewable energy sources help reduce carbon emissions."
)
```

6. Assemble and tidy a text collection from the `docs2` set, following the same procedure used previously.
7. Generate a document-term matrix (DTM) from this cleaned text and eliminate any rows representing documents with no remaining content. Indicate how many valid documents remain after this step.
8. Train a Latent Dirichlet Allocation (LDA) model on the resulting DTM, specifying two topics.
9. Retrieve the six most representative words associated with each topic. Compare these to the key terms found in the first dataset. What patterns, changes, or consistencies do you observe between the two?
10. Create a visual representation of the top five words per topic using a bar chart—consider using the `ggplot2` package for an effective display.

Dataset 3: Short Reviews on Movies and Books

R Code

```
docs3 <- c(
  "The movie had stunning visuals but a weak plot.",
  "I enjoyed the book's characters and writing style.",
  "The film's soundtrack was memorable and fitting.",
  "The novel explores complex themes in an engaging way.",
  "Both the book and movie left a lasting impression."
)
```

11. Process and sanitize the text data as done with earlier sets, then construct the corresponding document-term matrix.

12. Run a topic modeling algorithm (LDA) on this matrix, specifying that it should identify two distinct themes.

13. Identify the five most prominent terms associated with each discovered topic.

14. Use these terms to interpret and assign a meaningful label to each topic—e.g., categorize them as "Movie" or "Book" based on their content.

15. Reflect on how topic modeling methods like LDA can help distill large volumes of customer input (e.g., reviews or survey comments) into key themes or recurring issues.

Lab 12

Non-negative Matrix Factorization (NMF)

Non-negative Matrix Factorization (NMF) is another method we can use to find patterns in text, especially when we're looking for underlying topics. Like LDA, it helps break a bunch of documents into meaningful themes. But instead of relying on probabilities, NMF uses the actual word counts and splits them into two simpler parts: one that links words to topics, and another that links topics to documents. Since everything stays non-negative (no negative numbers), it's pretty straightforward to understand—higher numbers show stronger links. In this lab, we'll use a small example to see how NMF works and how it reveals topic patterns in a set of texts.

Lesson Steps

Step 1: Define a Word-Document Matrix

Let's start with a simple example: a small table showing how often certain words show up in a few short texts. In our case, we're using five words: cat, dog, apple, banana, and car, spread across three short documents. The first text is about pets, the second one is about fruit, and the third mixes pets with a mention of a car.

This setup makes it easier to see what NMF is doing behind the scenes. When we break the matrix down, we should start to see related words—like cat and dog, or apple and banana—grouping together into themes, while unrelated ones like car stand apart.

```r
# Define word-document matrix
A <- matrix(c(
  2, 0, 1,  # cat
  2, 0, 1,  # dog
  0, 2, 0,  # apple
  0, 2, 0,  # banana
  0, 0, 3   # car
), nrow = 5, byrow = TRUE)

rownames(A) <- c("cat", "dog", "apple", "banana", "car")
colnames(A) <- c("doc1", "doc2", "doc3")
A
```

```
##        doc1 doc2 doc3
## cat       2    0    1
## dog       2    0    1
## apple     0    2    0
## banana    0    2    0
## car       0    0    3
```

Step 2: Initialize W and H Matrices

To apply NMF, we initialize two matrices: W and H. The W matrix links words to topics, and the H matrix links topics to documents. Each row of W corresponds to a word, and each column corresponds to a topic. Higher values indicate a stronger connection between a word and a topic. Similarly, each row of H corresponds to a topic, and each column corresponds to a document, showing how much each topic contributes to that document.

In our case, we choose to model two topics. We might expect one topic to represent pets and another to represent fruits. "Cat" and "dog" are initially associated with the first topic, while "apple" and "banana" are associated with the second. The word "car" is given a small weight in the second topic as a placeholder. The H matrix then shows how much of each topic is present in each document. Document 1 is primarily about pets, document 2 about fruits, and document 3 contains some of both.

R Code

```
# Initialize W (words x topics)
W <- matrix(c(
  1, 0,    # cat
  1, 0,    # dog
  0, 1,    # apple
  0, 1,    # banana
  0, 0.5  # car
), nrow = 5, byrow = TRUE)

# Initialize H (topics x documents)
H <- matrix(c(
  2, 0, 1,    # topic 1
  0, 2, 1     # topic 2
), nrow = 2, byrow = TRUE)


cat("Matrix W:\n")
```

Output

```
## Matrix W:
```

R Code

```
print(W)
```

Output
```
##         [,1] [,2]
## [1,]     1   0.0
## [2,]     1   0.0
## [3,]     0   1.0
## [4,]     0   1.0
## [5,]     0   0.5
```

R Code
```
cat("\nMatrix H:\n")
```

Output
```
##
## Matrix H:
```

R Code
```
print(H)
```

Output
```
##      [,1] [,2] [,3]
## [1,]   2    0    1
## [2,]   0    2    1
```

Step 3: Perform a Single NMF Multiplicative Update

At first, W and H are only guesses. NMF improves these guesses through a process of iterative updates. In this step, we perform a single update using multiplicative rules. The idea is to compare the product of W and H (which we'll call WH) to the original matrix A. The closer WH is to A, the better our model is at explaining the data.

We first update the H matrix by adjusting it to better match the actual word counts in A. Then we recompute WH and use it to update the W matrix. Each update brings our estimate of the original matrix closer to the true values. Even though we perform just one round of updates in this lab for simplicity, real-world applications use many iterations to refine the result.

R Code

```
# Step 3: One NMF multiplicative update
epsilon <- 1e-9


# Update H
WH <- W %*% H
H_numer <- t(W) %*% A
H_denom <- t(W) %*% WH + epsilon
H <- H * (H_numer / H_denom)


# Update W
WH <- W %*% H
W_numer <- A %*% t(H)
W_denom <- WH %*% t(H) + epsilon
W <- W * (W_numer / W_denom)


cat("Update Matrix W:\n")
```

Output

```
## Update Matrix W:
```

R Code

```
print(W)
```

Output

```
##           [,1]        [,2]
## cat        1 0.0000000
## dog        1 0.0000000
## apple      0 0.9863014
## banana     0 0.9863014
## car        0 0.5547945
```

R Code

```
cat("\nUPdate Matrix H:\n")
```

Output

```
##
## UPdate Matrix H:
```

R Code

```
print(H)
```

Output

```
##      doc1     doc2      doc3
## [1,]    2 0.000000 1.0000000
## [2,]    0 1.777778 0.6666667
```

Step 4: View the Final Reconstructed Matrix

To see how well the NMF model captures the structure in our data, we multiply the updated W and H matrices. This product gives us a reconstructed version of the original matrix A. While it may not match the original values exactly, it shows how much the model has learned about the hidden structure—how often it expects each word to appear in each document based on the discovered topics.

R Code

```
# Final approximation
cat("\nReconstructed A   W %*% H:\n")
```

Output

```
##
## Reconstructed A   W %*% H:
```

R Code

```
print(round(W %*% H, 2))
```

Output

```
##           doc1 doc2 doc3
## cat          2 0.00 1.00
## dog          2 0.00 1.00
## apple        0 1.75 0.66
## banana       0 1.75 0.66
## car          0 0.99 0.37
```

The reconstructed matrix shows that "cat" and "dog" are estimated to appear twice in document 1 and once in document 3, while "apple" and "banana" appear only in document 2. The word "car" appears primarily in document 3. This matches our expectations and shows that NMF has successfully uncovered the topic structure in this small dataset.

Wrap-Up

This lab showed how NMF can find topics in text without needing labels. We started with a word-document table, split it into two parts—words to topics and topics to documents—and then combined them to see how well they captured the original data.

NMF is useful for spotting themes in large text collections. It groups related words and shows how those themes appear across different documents, which helps in tasks like search, recommendations, and analyzing feedback.

Exercise

Non-negative Matrix Factorization (NMF)

This exercise practice interpreting NMF and its outputs.

Dataset 1: Word-Document Matrix (Travel, Food, and Vehicles)

```
R Code
# Define word-document matrix
B <- matrix(c(
  3, 0, 0, # beach
  2, 0, 1, # airplane
  0, 4, 0, # pizza
  0, 3, 0, # pasta
  1, 0, 5 # car
), nrow = 5, byrow = TRUE)

rownames(B) <- c(
  "beach", "airplane", "pizza",
  "pasta", "car"
)
colnames(B) <- c("doc1", "doc2", "doc3")
B
```

Output

```
##            doc1 doc2 doc3
## beach         3    0    0
## airplane      2    0    1
## pizza         0    4    0
## pasta         0    3    0
## car           1    0    5
```

1. What are the names of the rows and columns in matrix B?
2. Looking at document 2, which word shows up the most?
3. Add up all the times the word "car" appears—what's the total across all documents?
4. Based on the word counts, which document seems to be about travel? What clues support your answer?
5. In document 3, how many different words appear at least once?

Dataset 2: Initial Matrices W and H for NMF (2 topics)

R Code

```
# Initialize W (words x topics)
W2 <- matrix(c(
  1, 0,    # beach
  1, 0,    # airplane
  0, 1,    # pizza
  0, 1,    # pasta
  0, 0.5   # car
), nrow = 5, byrow = TRUE)


# Initialize H (topics x documents)
H2 <- matrix(c(
  3, 0, 1,   # topic 1
  0, 4, 0    # topic 2
), nrow = 2, byrow = TRUE)


W2
```

Output

```
##       [,1] [,2]
## [1,]    1  0.0
## [2,]    1  0.0
## [3,]    0  1.0
## [4,]    0  1.0
## [5,]    0  0.5
```

R Code

```
H2
```

Output

```
##         [,1] [,2] [,3]
## [1,]    3    0    1
## [2,]    0    4    0
```

6. What kind of topic does the first column in W2 seem to describe?
7. In the last row of W2, the value for "car" is 0.5. What does that tell you?
8. Based on H2, which document has the most content related to topic 2?
9. Multiply W2 and H2. What does the result show you?
10. Why would you keep updating W2 and H2 over and over again to improve the model?

Lab 13

Latent Semantic Analysis

Introduction

Latent Semantic Analysis (LSA) is a powerful technique used to discover hidden patterns and themes within a collection of documents. By examining the relationships between words and documents, LSA helps reveal the main ideas underlying a set of texts. It does this by creating a matrix that counts word frequencies across documents and then applying a mathematical method called Singular Value Decomposition to reduce this matrix into a smaller set of key "concepts" that represent the core topics.

Unlike other methods such as Latent Dirichlet Allocation (LDA), which models documents as mixtures of topics using probability, LSA relies purely on linear algebra without probabilistic assumptions. Another related approach, Non-negative Matrix Factorization (NMF), also uses matrix factorization but restricts values to be positive, often resulting in more interpretable, parts-based themes.

In this introduction, we will explore how LSA works, how it compares to LDA and NMF, and why it is a useful tool for uncovering the hidden structure in textual data.

Lesson Steps

Step 1: Install Packages and Create Data

This code installs and loads the necessary R packages for text analysis and LSA modelling.

```
R Code
# Install if not already installed
options(repos = c(CRAN = "https://cran.r-project.org"))


install.packages("tm")
install.packages("lsa")
install.packages("SnowballC")


# Load libraries
library(tm)
library(lsa)
library(SnowballC)
```

This defines a small list of example sentences (documents) to be used in a simple text mining and topic modeling task.

```
R Code
# Step 1: Sample documents
documents <- c(
  "Cats are small furry animals.",
  "Dogs are loyal and friendly.",
  "Cats and dogs are popular pets.",
  "Birds can fly high in the sky.",
  "Many pets like cats and dogs live in homes."
)
```

Step 2: Preprocess the Text

This section creates a text corpus (a collection of documents) and prepares it for analysis by cleaning the text. It converts all words to lowercase, removes punctuation, numbers, and common stopwords (like "the", "and", "is"). It also applies stemming to reduce words to their root form (e.g., "animals" becomes "anim"), and removes any extra whitespace.

```
R Code
# Step 2: Preprocess the text
corpus <- Corpus(VectorSource(documents))
corpus <- tm_map(corpus, content_transformer(tolower))
corpus <- tm_map(corpus, removePunctuation)
corpus <- tm_map(corpus, removeNumbers)
corpus <- tm_map(corpus, removeWords,
                 stopwords("english"))
corpus <- tm_map(corpus, stemDocument)
corpus <- tm_map(corpus, stripWhitespace)
```

Preprocessing helps reduce noise and make the text easier to analyze for meaningful patterns.

Step 3: Create Term-Document Matrix

In this step, we make a table that shows how often each word shows up in each document. Words go down the rows, documents go across the columns, and the numbers tell us how many times each word appears. Turning it into a matrix lets us do analytics with it more easily.

```
R Code
# Step 3: Create term-document matrix
tdm <- TermDocumentMatrix(corpus)
tdm_matrix <- as.matrix(tdm)
```

The TDM is essential because it turns raw text into a structured numeric format that LSA (and other algorithms) can analyze to find patterns or topics.

Step 4: Apply LSA

In this step, we apply the lsa() function to the term-document matrix. Latent Semantic Analysis (LSA) helps by taking the large table of word counts and turning it into a smaller set of main topics or ideas. This reduces the complexity of the data, making it easier to see the underlying themes in the documents.

```
R Code
# Step 4: Apply LSA
lsa_result <- lsa(tdm_matrix, dim = 2)
```

The argument dim = 2 tells LSA to keep only the top two most important concepts, capturing the main patterns in the data. This reduction is done using Singular Value Decomposition (SVD), which breaks the matrix into parts to reveal structure.

By simplifying the data in this way, LSA helps us find hidden relationships between words and documents. Using just 2 dimensions keeps the results easy to understand, which is ideal for small datasets like this one.

Step 5: View Results

This step shows the results of the LSA by printing two tables: the document-topic matrix and the term-topic matrix.

R Code
```
# Step 5: View results
cat("Document-topic matrix:\n")
```

Output
```
## Document-topic matrix:
```

R Code
```
print(round(lsa_result$dk, 2))
```

Output
```
##      [,1] [,2]
## 1 -0.24    0
## 2 -0.20    0
## 3 -0.52    0
## 4  0.00   -1
## 5 -0.80    0
```

This output shows how each of the five documents relates to the two main topics discovered by LSA. The matrix has two columns, one for each topic, and five rows, one for each document. The values in the matrix represent how strongly each document is connected to each topic.

For example, Document 1 has a value of -0.24 in Topic 1 and 0 in Topic 2, meaning it is somewhat related to Topic 1 and not at all to Topic 2. Documents 1, 2, 3, and 5 all have negative values in Topic 1 and zero in Topic 2. This suggests they are grouped together under the same theme—likely the one about pets.

Document 4 stands out with a value of -1.00 in Topic 2 and 0 in Topic 1, indicating it is strongly associated with a different topic—birds and flying.

LSA has successfully separated the documents into two distinct topics: one for pets (cats and dogs), and one for birds.

R Code
```
cat("\nTerm-topic matrix:\n")
```

Output
```
##
## Term-topic matrix:
```

R Code
```
print(round(lsa_result$tk, 2))
```

```
Output
##              [,1]   [,2]
## anim     -0.08   0.00
## cat      -0.50   0.00
## furri    -0.08   0.00
## small    -0.08   0.00
## dog      -0.49   0.00
## friend   -0.07   0.00
## loyal    -0.07   0.00
## pet      -0.43   0.00
## popular  -0.17   0.00
## bird      0.00  -0.45
## can       0.00  -0.45
## fli       0.00  -0.45
## high      0.00  -0.45
## sky       0.00  -0.45
## home     -0.26   0.00
## like     -0.26   0.00
## live     -0.26   0.00
## mani     -0.26   0.00
```

This term-topic matrix shows how each word contributes to the two topics identified by LSA. Each row represents a word, and each column represents a topic.

Words like "cat" (-0.50), "dog" (-0.49), "pet" (-0.43), and "home", "live", "like" (around -0.26) have strong values in Topic 1 and 0 in Topic 2. These clearly relate to domestic animals and suggest Topic 1 is about pets.

Words like "bird", "can", "fli", "high", and "sky" have strong negative values in Topic 2 and 0 in Topic 1, indicating they are exclusively tied to

Topic 2—birds and flying.

In summary, Topic 1 is about pets (cats, dogs, and home life) and Topic 2 is about birds and flying.

The sign of the values doesn't indicate sentiment—just position in the topic space. The size (magnitude) of the number shows how strongly a word or document is related to a topic.

Wrap-Up

In this lab, we explored how Latent Semantic Analysis (LSA) helps find hidden patterns in text. By breaking down the original word-document table into a smaller set of concepts, LSA reveals the main ideas that link documents and words together.

Using our example, we saw how LSA takes complex text data and turns it into clear topics, grouping related documents and highlighting important words for each theme. This makes it easier to spot connections that aren't obvious just from counting words.

Overall, the lab showed that LSA is a solid way to uncover underlying themes in text. It's a useful tool for digging into text collections, helping with tasks like searching, summarizing, and exploring data. Knowing how LSA works gives you a good base for using it on bigger and more complicated text sets to find meaningful insights.

Lab 6-3 Exercises

Latent Semantic Analysis

In these exercises yhou will apply LSA to different text datasets, analyze the results, and answer questions that deepen your understanding of how LSA uncovers topics.

Dataset 1: Sports and Weather Documents

Create the following small dataset of 5 documents related to sports and weather.

```
R Code
documents1 <- c(
  "Football players run on the field.",
  "The rain is heavy today.",
  "Basketball is popular in many countries.",
  "It is sunny with a light breeze.",
  "Many fans watch the soccer game."
)
```

1. Take the `documents1` collection and clean it up: change all letters to lowercase, get rid of punctuation and numbers, remove common words like "the" or "and," and simplify words to their base form. Then, show what the cleaned-up text looks like.
2. Build a table that shows how often each word appears in each document using the cleaned text. Display this table as a matrix.
3. Use Latent Semantic Analysis (LSA) on this table, asking it to reduce the data into two main concepts. Print out the results showing how each document relates to these concepts.
4. Look at the results and say which documents seem to share the same

167

main idea. Explain your thoughts in plain language.

5. Show the table that links words to topics. Point out which words are most strongly connected to the first topic and which belong to the second.

Dataset 2: Food and Technology Documents

Create a second dataset of 5 documents about food and technology.

```
R Code
documents2 <- c(
  "Smartphones have advanced cameras.",
  "Cooking pasta requires boiling water.",
  "Many people use laptops daily.",
  "Baking bread needs precise timing.",
  "Technology improves communication."
)
```

6. Clean up `documents2` just like you did with Dataset 1, then display the cleaned text.

7. Make a term-document matrix from this cleaned text and show it in matrix form.

8. Run LSA on the matrix using two topics and display how each document relates to those topics.

9. From the document-topic results, say which documents seem to belong together and why.

10. Look at the term-topic matrix and list some important words tied to each topic.

Lab 14

Naive Bayes Text Classification

Naive Bayes is one of the simplest and fastest text classification methods. It's based on probability and uses something called Bayes' Theorem. The word naive means it assumes that all the words in a text are independent of each other — which isn't true in real life, but it still works surprisingly well.

Naive Bayes counts how often each word appears in texts from different categories (like spam vs. not spam), and then uses those counts to guess what category a new message belongs to. It's great when you have a small dataset or want something that runs quickly.

Lesson Steps

Step 1: Install and load required packages

This step installs and loads the necessary R packages for text processing (tm and SnowballC) and for building the Naive Bayes classifier (e1071).

```
R Code
# Install if not already installed
options(repos = c(CRAN = "https://cran.r-project.org"))

install.packages("tm")
install.packages("e1071")
install.packages("SnowballC")

library(tm)
library(e1071)
library(SnowballC)
```

Step 2: Create sample text data and labels

This step creates a small sample dataset made up of six short text documents about either sports or science. Each document is paired with a label that indicates its category, which the model will use for learning.

```
R Code
texts <- c(
  "The football team won the championship",
  "He scored a goal in the match",
  "Basketball is a popular sport",
  "Physics explains the laws of motion",
  "She studied chemistry for the exam",
  "Biology is the study of life"
)

labels <- c("sports", "sports", "sports",
            "science", "science", "science")
```

Step 3: Clean and preprocess the text

In this step, we get the raw text ready for analysis by cleaning it up. We start by putting all the documents together into a collection called a corpus, which makes it easier to work with the text using R's tm package. Then, we clean each document to remove things that might get in the way.

First, we change all the letters to lowercase so words like "Team" and "team" are counted the same. Next, we take out punctuation and numbers because they usually don't help with understanding the text. After that, we remove common words like "the," "is," and "and" since they don't add much meaning. Then, we simplify words by chopping them down to their base form—for example, "scoring," "scored," and "scores" all become "score." Finally, we clean up any extra spaces that might be left over.

171

R Code

```
# Create a text corpus from the documents
corpus <- VCorpus(VectorSource(texts))

# Convert all text to lowercase
corpus <- tm_map(corpus, content_transformer(tolower))

# Remove punctuation marks
corpus <- tm_map(corpus, removePunctuation)

# Remove numbers
corpus <- tm_map(corpus, removeNumbers)

# Remove common English stopwords
corpus <- tm_map(corpus, removeWords,
                 stopwords("english"))

# Reduce words to their root form
corpus <- tm_map(corpus, stemDocument)

# Eliminate extra whitespace
corpus <- tm_map(corpus, stripWhitespace)

# View cleaned text after preprocessing
for (i in 1:length(corpus)) {
  cat(paste("Document", i, ":\n"))
  cat(as.character(corpus[[i]]), "\n\n")
}
```

Output
```
## Document 1 :
## footbal team won championship
##
## Document 2 :
## score goal match
##
## Document 3 :
## basketbal popular sport
##
## Document 4 :
## physic explain law motion
##
## Document 5 :
## studi chemistri exam
##
## Document 6 :
## biolog studi life
```

Step 4: Create a Document-Term Matrix

Now, we turn the cleaned text into a Document-Term Matrix, or DTM for short. This is basically a table that turns words into numbers so computers can work with the text. In the table, each row stands for one document, and each column is a unique word from all the documents combined. The numbers inside show how often each word appears in each document.

R Code
```
dtm <- DocumentTermMatrix(corpus)
```

Step 5: Prepare data frame for modeling

To get the data ready for modeling, we first turn the document-term matrix into a regular table. Using as.matrix(dtm) changes it from a sparse format to a full matrix, and then as.data.frame() makes it into a table where each row is a document and each column is a word. After that, we add a new column called label to show the category each document belongs to.

```
R Code
data <- as.data.frame(as.matrix(dtm))
data$label <- labels


head(data[,1:6])
```

```
Output
##    basketbal biolog championship chemistri exam explain
## 1          0      0            1         0    0       0
## 2          0      0            0         0    0       0
## 3          1      0            0         0    0       0
## 4          0      0            0         0    0       1
## 5          0      0            0         1    1       0
## 6          0      1            0         0    0       0
```

```
R Code
head(data[,7:12])
```

Output

```
##    footbal goal law life match motion
## 1        1    0   0    0     0      0
## 2        0    1   0    0     1      0
## 3        0    0   0    0     0      0
## 4        0    0   1    0     0      1
## 5        0    0   0    0     0      0
## 6        0    0   0    1     0      0
```

R Code

```
head(data[,13:18])
```

Output

```
##    physic popular score sport studi team
## 1       0       0     0     0     0    1
## 2       0       0     1     0     0    0
## 3       0       1     0     1     0    0
## 4       1       0     0     0     0    0
## 5       0       0     0     0     1    0
## 6       0       0     0     0     1    0
```

This output shows the first 6 rows of the processed dataset. Each row represents one document, and each column (except the last one) represents a unique word. The final column, label, shows the category assigned to each document. This labeled format is essential for training a supervised machine learning model.

Step 6: Split data into training and test sets

We split the data into two parts: one for training the model and one for testing it. The line `train_data <- data[1:4, ]` selects the first 4 documents to use as the training set. The line `test_data <- data[5:6, ]` selects the remaining 2 documents to use as the test set.

Next, we extract the true labels for the test documents using `test_labels <- test_data$label`. This saves the actual categories so we can later compare them to the model's predictions. Finally, `test_data$label <- NULL` removes the label column from the test input, ensuring the model doesn't "cheat" by seeing the correct answers during prediction.

```
R Code
train_data <- data[1:4, ]   # First 4 for training
test_data <- data[5:6, ]    # Last 2 for testing
test_labels <- test_data$label
test_data$label <- NULL     # Remove label column from test set
```

Step 7: Train Naive Bayes model

We train a Naive Bayes classification model using the training data. The function `naiveBayes(label ~ ., data = train_data)` tells R to build a model where the label column is the target variable and all the other columns are the features used to predict that label.

```
R Code
model <- naiveBayes(label ~ ., data = train_data)
```

Step 8: Predict on test data

We use the trained Naive Bayes model to make predictions on the test data. The line `predictions <- predict(model, test_data)` runs the model on the test set and returns the predicted labels for each test document.

```
R Code
predictions <- predict(model, test_data)
```

Step 9: Show predicted vs actual labels

We compare the model's predictions to the actual labels from the test data to see how well it performed. The line `print(data.frame(Predicted = predictions, Actual = test_labels))` displays a small table with two columns: the predicted category and the true category for each test document.

```
R Code
print(data.frame(Predicted = predictions,
                 Actual = test_labels))
```

```
Output
##    Predicted  Actual
## 1     sports science
## 2     sports science
```

The model predicted both test documents as "sports," but the actual labels were "science," indicating that it misclassified both examples. This is not a good result, but this is a pedagogical example using a very small dataset. In practice, larger and more diverse datasets are necessary to train accurate models.

Wrap Up

In this lab, we explored how the Naive Bayes algorithm uses probability to classify text documents in a simple and fast way. Even though it assumes words appear independently—which isn't really true in everyday language—Naive Bayes often works well, especially with smaller datasets or when you need quick results.

We went through the whole process: cleaning and preparing the text, turning it into numbers with a Document-Term Matrix, training the model with labeled data, and then using it to guess the categories of new documents. While the small dataset caused some mistakes, the lab helped us understand the main ideas and steps behind using Naive Bayes for text classification.

In short, this exercise shows that Naive Bayes is a solid starting point in text mining and language processing, giving a good base to build more advanced tools and applications.

Exercises

Naive Bayes Text Classification

Naive Bayes is a simple, fast, and effective method for text classification that assumes word independence. In this exercise set, you will create labeled text datasets, preprocess the data, build Naive Bayes models, and interpret the results.

Dataset 1: Movie Reviews (Positive / Negative)

Create this dataset of 6 short movie review texts and their sentiment labels.

```
R Code
texts1 <- c(
  "I loved the thrilling action scenes",
  "The movie was boring and too long",
  "Amazing story and fantastic acting",
  "Poor direction and weak plot",
  "A wonderful experience from start to finish",
  "Not worth watching, very dull"
)

labels1 <- c("positive", "negative", "positive",
             "negative", "positive", "negative")
```

1. Start by cleaning up `texts1`: make everything lowercase, take out punctuation, numbers, common filler words, and shorten words to their roots. Also, remove extra spaces. Then show what the cleaned-up texts look like.

2. From that cleaned collection, build a table showing how often each word appears in each text. Display this table as a matrix.

179

3. Turn this matrix into a regular data frame and add a new column for the labels. Show the first few rows of this table.

4. Split the data into two groups—use the first four rows for training the model and the last two for testing. Show the size of each group.

5. Use the training data to build a Naive Bayes classifier. Then predict the labels for the test set and compare the predictions to the real labels.

Dataset 2: Tech Gadget Reviews (Good / Bad)

Create a second dataset of 6 short texts about technology gadgets and their quality labels.

```
R Code
texts2 <- c(
  "The smartphone has an excellent battery life",
  "Terrible customer service and buggy software",
  "Fast processor and crisp display",
  "Poor build quality and frequent crashes",
  "Highly recommend this new tablet",
  "Disappointed with the sound quality"
)

labels2 <- c("good", "bad", "good", "bad", "good", "bad")
```

6. Clean up `texts2` just like you did with Dataset 1. Show the cleaned texts.

7. Make a document-term matrix from the cleaned text and display it as a matrix.

8. Convert that matrix into a data frame, add the labels in a new column, and show the first few rows.

9. Split the data into training (first four rows) and test sets (last two rows). Show the size of each set.

10. Build a Naive Bayes model using the training data, then predict the labels for the test set. Show the predicted and actual labels and give a quick comment on how well the model did.

Lab 15

Support Vector Machine (SVM) for Text Classification

Support Vector Machine (SVM) is a powerful classification algorithm that works well with complex data. It tries to find the best boundary, called a hyperplane, that separates different groups or classes of data points with the largest margin.

In text classification, SVM looks at features derived from text, such as word counts, and learns how to separate documents into categories, like positive or negative sentiment. This lab demonstrates how to use SVM to classify short movie reviews as either positive or negative sentiment containing.

Lesson Steps

Step 1: Install and load required packages

We will use several R packages. The first one is `tm`, which helps with text mining tasks such as cleaning and preparing text data. The second is `e1071`, which provides the implementation of the SVM algorithm. The third package is `SnowballC`, which is used for stemming words by reducing them to their root forms.

Load and install these.

```
R Code
# Install if not already installed
options(repos = c(CRAN = "https://cran.r-project.org"))
# Step 1: Install and load required packages
# Uncomment if needed
install.packages("tm")
install.packages("e1071")
install.packages("SnowballC")


library(tm)
library(e1071)
library(SnowballC)
```

Step 2: Create sample text data and labels

We create a small dataset of six short movie review sentences. Each sentence is labeled as either positive or negative sentiment. The texts vector contains the sentences, and the labels vector holds the true sentiment category for each text, which we will use for supervised learning.

```
R Code
# Step 2: Create sample text data and labels
texts <- c(
  "I loved the movie, it was fantastic and thrilling",
  "The film was boring and too long",
  "What a great performance by the lead actor",
  "I did not enjoy the plot, it was predictable",
  "An amazing story with brilliant acting",
  "Terrible movie, I would not recommend it"
)

labels <- c("positive", "negative", "positive",
            "negative", "positive", "negative")
```

Step 3: Clean and preprocess the text

Standard preprocessing text procedures are applied here.

R Code

```
# Step 3: Clean and preprocess the text


# Create a corpus from the texts
corpus <- VCorpus(VectorSource(texts))


# Convert all text to lowercase
corpus <- tm_map(corpus, content_transformer(tolower))


# Remove punctuation marks
corpus <- tm_map(corpus, removePunctuation)


# Remove numbers from the text
corpus <- tm_map(corpus, removeNumbers)


# Remove common stopwords like "the" and "and"
corpus <- tm_map(corpus, removeWords, stopwords("english"))


# Reduce words to their stem/root form
corpus <- tm_map(corpus, stemDocument)


# Remove extra whitespace
corpus <- tm_map(corpus, stripWhitespace)


# Show the first few cleaned documents to see the result
inspect(corpus[1:3])
```

```
Output
## <<VCorpus>>
## Metadata:  corpus specific: 0, document level (indexed): 0
## Content:  documents: 3
##
## [[1]]
## <<PlainTextDocument>>
## Metadata:  7
## Content:  chars: 24
##
## [[2]]
## <<PlainTextDocument>>
## Metadata:  7
## Content:  chars: 14
##
## [[3]]
## <<PlainTextDocument>>
## Metadata:  7
## Content:  chars: 24
```

Step 4: Create a Document-Term Matrix (DTM)

The Document-Term Matrix represents the corpus as a matrix where each row corresponds to a document (each review), and each column corresponds to a unique word or term that appears across all documents. Each cell in the matrix contains the frequency count of the term in the document. This numeric matrix is the main input feature set for machine learning because it converts text into numbers that the SVM can work with.

187

R Code
```
# Step 4: Create a Document-Term Matrix
dtm <- DocumentTermMatrix(corpus)


# Show a small sample of the DTM
inspect(dtm[1:4, 1:8])
```

Output
```
## <<DocumentTermMatrix (documents: 4, terms: 8)>>
## Non-/sparse entries: 5/27
## Sparsity             : 84%
## Maximal term length: 9
## Weighting            : term frequency (tf)
## Sample               :
##        Terms
## Docs act actor amaz bore brilliant enjoy fantast film
##    1   0    0    0    0         0     0       1    0
##    2   0    0    0    1         0     0       0    1
##    3   0    1    0    0         0     0       0    0
##    4   0    0    0    0         0     1       0    0
```

Step 5: Convert to data frame and add labels

The sparse matrix from the Document-Term Matrix is converted into a regular data frame for easier manipulation. The sentiment labels are then added to the data frame as a new column called `label`. The data frame now contains columns for the word counts and a column for the sentiment category.

188

R Code

```
# Step 5: Convert to data frame and add labels
data <- as.data.frame(as.matrix(dtm))
data$label <- labels

# Show first few rows of the data frame
print(head(data[,1:9]))
```

Output

##	act	actor	amaz	bore	brilliant	enjoy	fantast	film	great
## 1	0	0	0	0	0	0	1	0	0
## 2	0	0	0	1	0	0	0	1	0
## 3	0	1	0	0	0	0	0	0	1
## 4	0	0	0	0	0	1	0	0	0
## 5	1	0	1	0	1	0	0	0	0
## 6	0	0	0	0	0	0	0	0	0

R Code

```
print(head(data[,10:16]))
```

Output

```
##    lead long love movi perform plot predict
## 1    0    0    1    1       0    0       0
## 2    0    1    0    0       0    0       0
## 3    1    0    0    0       1    0       0
## 4    0    0    0    0       0    1       1
## 5    0    0    0    0       0    0       0
## 6    0    0    0    1       0    0       0
```

R Code

```
print(head(data[,17:19]))
```

Output

```
##    recommend stori terribl
## 1       0      0      0
## 2       0      0      0
## 3       0      0      0
## 4       0      0      0
## 5       0      1      0
## 6       1      0      1
```

The SVM model expects a data frame with predictor variables and a target label, so this prepares the data in the correct format.

Step 6: Split into training and test sets

We split the data into two parts. The first four reviews will be used as the training set to build the model, while the last two reviews will be used as the test set to evaluate how well the model performs on new data. The true labels of the test set are kept separately for evaluation. The label column is removed from the test data to prevent information leakage during prediction.

R Code
```
# Step 6: Split into training and test sets
train_data <- data[1:4, ]
test_data <- data[5:6, ]
test_labels <- test_data$label



# Remove label from test features
test_data$label <- NULL
```

This ensures that the model is trained only on the training data and tested independently.

Step 7: Train the SVM model

The SVM classifier is trained on the training data. The `label` column is converted to a factor because it represents categorical classes. A linear kernel is used because it often performs well for text classification when working with document-term matrices.

R Code
```
# Step 7: Train SVM model
train_data$label <- as.factor(train_data$label)
model <- svm(label ~ ., data = train_data,
             kernel = "linear")
```

The SVM algorithm learns the best hyperplane that separates positive and negative reviews based on word frequencies.

Step 8: Make predictions on test data

The trained SVM model is applied to the test data to predict sentiment labels for the unseen reviews.

```
R Code
# Step 8: Make predictions on test data
predictions <- predict(model, test_data)
```

The model assigns each test document a predicted class label.

Step 9: Compare predictions with actual labels

The predicted labels are compared with the true sentiment labels to evaluate performance. This comparison helps us understand how accurately the model classifies new documents.

```
R Code
# Step 9: Compare predictions with actual labels
print(data.frame(Predicted = predictions,
                 Actual = test_labels))
```

```
Output
##    Predicted    Actual
## 5   negative  positive
## 6   positive  negative
```

This output shows which test reviews were classified correctly and which were misclassified.

With this example, the SVM model should be able to correctly identify the sentiment of the test reviews, assuming the training set captures the key features well. Because the training dataset is small, the results here are illustrative rather than definitive. Real-world models require larger, more diverse data for reliable performance.

Wrap-Up

This lab demonstrated how to use Support Vector Machines for text classification by transforming raw movie reviews into a format suitable for machine learning and then training an SVM to predict sentiment labels. Although the example used a small dataset for simplicity, the steps are the foundation for applying SVMs to larger real-world text classification problems.

Exercises

Support Vector Machine (SVM) for Text Classification

This exercise set lets you practice text classification using Support Vector Machines (SVM).

Dataset 1: Customer Feedback on Electronics

```
R Code
# Dataset 1: Electronics product reviews
texts1 <- c(
  "The battery life is excellent and lasts all day",
  "Poor sound quality and too much static noise",
  "Amazing camera, pictures are sharp and clear",
  "The screen freezes frequently, very frustrating",
  "Great value for the price, highly recommend",
  "Terrible build quality, broke after one week"
)

labels1 <- c("positive", "negative", "positive",
             "negative", "positive", "negative")
```

1. After cleaning `texts1` by making everything lowercase, removing punctuation, numbers, common words, and reducing words to their roots, show the cleaned texts.
2. Build a Document-Term Matrix (DTM) from this cleaned text and display the first 4 rows and 6 columns.
3. Turn the DTM into a data frame, add the labels, and show the first 6 rows.
4. Split the data into two parts: use the first 4 reviews to train the model

and the last 2 to test it. Show the labels for both sets.

5. Train a support vector machine (SVM) model with a linear kernel on the training data, then predict the labels for the test reviews. Compare the predicted labels to the actual ones.

Dataset 2: Tweets About Food

```
R Code
# Dataset 2: Food-related tweets
texts2 <- c(
  "Loved the spicy tacos at the new restaurant!",
  "The pasta was undercooked and bland",
  "Delicious desserts and friendly staff",
  "Waited 30 minutes for cold soup, disappointing",
  "Best pizza in town, will come again",
  "Rude waiter and slow service"
)

labels2 <- c("positive", "negative", "positive",
             "negative", "positive", "negative")
```

6. Clean the texts in `texts2` just like before and show the first three cleaned documents.

7. Create a Document-Term Matrix from the cleaned texts and tell us its size (how many rows and columns it has).

8. Turn the DTM into a data frame, add the labels, and show how the sentiment labels are spread out.

9. Train a support vector machine using a linear kernel on the first four tweets, then test it on the last two. Show the confusion matrix that compares the predicted labels to the actual ones.

10. Try using a radial kernel (kernal='radial') instead of linear, retrain the

195

model, and compare how the predictions change between the two.

Lab 16

Logistic Regression for Text Classification

Introduction

Logistic Regression is a common method used for classification tasks. Unlike linear regression it is not used for predicting numeric values but for predicting categories. In text classification, logistic regression calculates the probability that a given text belongs to a certain class, such as positive or negative sentiment, based on the presence or absence of words.

For example, it might calculate there is a 90% chance that a sentence is about sports. If that probability is higher than 50%, the text is classified as "sports." Logistic regression is simple, interpretable, and often effective.

Lesson Steps

Step 1: Install and load required packages

We will use the `tm` package for text mining and the `SnowballC` package for word stemming to preprocess and analyze text data.

R Code
```
# Uncomment these lines if packages are not installed
install.packages("tm")
```

Output
```
## Error in install.packages : Updating loaded packages
```

R Code
```
install.packages("SnowballC")
```

Output
```
## Error in install.packages : Updating loaded packages
```

R Code
```
library(tm)           # Text mining
library(SnowballC)    # Word stemming
```

Step 2: Create sample text data and labels

We create a small dataset of 10 text samples, each labeled as "positive" or "negative" sentiment. This labeled data will be used to train and evaluate the classification model.

R Code

```
texts <- c(
  "I absolutely loved the movie!",
  "What a fantastic performance by the lead actor.",
  "The meal was delicious and well-presented.",
  "I'm so happy with the customer service.",
  "The book was inspiring and beautifully written.",
  "The product broke on the first day.",
  "It was a terrible experience overall.",
  "I am very disappointed with this purchase.",
  "The service was awful and rude.",
  "Nothing worked as expected, complete waste of money."
)

labels <- c(
  "positive", "positive", "positive", "positive",
  "positive","negative", "negative", "negative",
  "negative", "negative"
)
```

Step 3: Clean and preprocess the text

We create a text corpus and clean it by converting to lowercase, removing punctuation and numbers, removing stopwords (common words with little meaning), stemming words to their root form, and stripping extra whitespace. These steps simplify the text to improve the model's effectiveness.

R Code

```r
# Create a text corpus from the raw texts
corpus <- VCorpus(VectorSource(texts))


# Convert all text to lowercase
corpus <- tm_map(corpus, content_transformer(tolower))


# Remove punctuation marks
corpus <- tm_map(corpus, removePunctuation)


# Remove numbers from the text
corpus <- tm_map(corpus, removeNumbers)


# Remove common stopwords like "the" and "and"
corpus <- tm_map(corpus, removeWords, stopwords("english"))


# Reduce words to their stem/root form
corpus <- tm_map(corpus, stemDocument)


# Remove extra whitespace
corpus <- tm_map(corpus, stripWhitespace)


# Display the first three cleaned documents to check results
inspect(corpus[1:3])
```

```
Output
## <<VCorpus>>
## Metadata:  corpus specific: 0, document level (indexed): 0
## Content:   documents: 3
##
## [[1]]
## <<PlainTextDocument>>
## Metadata:  7
## Content:   chars: 17
##
## [[2]]
## <<PlainTextDocument>>
## Metadata:  7
## Content:   chars: 26
##
## [[3]]
## <<PlainTextDocument>>
## Metadata:  7
## Content:   chars: 20
```

Step 4: Create Document-Term Matrix

We convert the cleaned text corpus into a Document-Term Matrix (DTM). Each row corresponds to a text document and each column corresponds to a unique word (term). Values represent the frequency of each word in each document, turning text into numeric data for the model.

R Code

```
dtm <- DocumentTermMatrix(corpus)


# Show a small sample of DTM entries
inspect(dtm[1:4, 1:6])
```

Output

```
## <<DocumentTermMatrix (documents: 4, terms: 6)>>
## Non-/sparse entries: 2/22
## Sparsity            : 92%
## Maximal term length: 7
## Weighting           : term frequency (tf)
## Sample              :
##      Terms
## Docs absolut actor beauti book broke complet
##    1       1     0      0    0     0       0
##    2       0     1      0    0     0       0
##    3       0     0      0    0     0       0
##    4       0     0      0    0     0       0
```

Step 5: Convert to data frame and add labels

We convert the sparse DTM into a regular data frame for easier handling. We also add the sentiment labels to this data frame, pairing the input features (word frequencies) with their corresponding output labels.

R Code

```
data <- as.data.frame(as.matrix(dtm))
data$label <- labels


#Show first few columns and labels
data[,1:5]
```

Output

```
##      absolut actor beauti book broke
## 1         1     0      0    0     0
## 2         0     1      0    0     0
## 3         0     0      0    0     0
## 4         0     0      0    0     0
## 5         0     0      1    1     0
## 6         0     0      0    0     1
## 7         0     0      0    0     0
## 8         0     0      0    0     0
## 9         0     0      0    0     0
## 10        0     0      0    0     0
```

R Code

```
data[,32:34]
```

Output			
##	work	written	label
## 1	0	0	positive
## 2	0	0	positive
## 3	0	0	positive
## 4	0	0	positive
## 5	0	1	positive
## 6	0	0	negative
## 7	0	0	negative
## 8	0	0	negative
## 9	0	0	negative
## 10	1	0	negative

Step 6: Split into training and test sets (80% training, 20% test)

To evaluate the model fairly, we split the data into training and test sets. We use 80% of the data for training and 20% for testing. Setting a seed ensures reproducibility. We separate labels from test inputs to simulate real prediction conditions.

R Code

```
set.seed(42)
# 80% for training
train_index <- sample(1:nrow(data), 0.8 * nrow(data))
train_data <- data[train_index, ]
test_data <- data[-train_index, ]
test_labels <- test_data$label
test_data$label <- NULL


print("Training data labels:")
```

Output

```
## [1] "Training data labels:"
```

R Code

```
print(table(train_data$label))
```

Output

```
##
## negative positive
##        4        4
```

R Code

```
print("Test data labels:")
```

Output
```
## [1] "Test data labels:"
```

R Code
```
print(table(test_labels))
```

Output
```
## test_labels
## negative positive
##        1        1
```

Step 7: Train logistic regression model

We convert the label column in the training data to a factor, which is required for classification. Then, we train a logistic regression model using all word features to predict the sentiment label.

R Code
```
train_data$label <- as.factor(train_data$label)
model <- glm(label ~ ., data = train_data,
             family = "binomial")


# Show model summary coefficients
summary(model)$coefficients
```

Output

```
##                    Estimate Std. Error       z value  Pr(>|z|)
## (Intercept) -2.456607e+01    131010.7 -1.875119e-04 0.9998504
## absolut       4.913214e+01    185277.2  2.651818e-04 0.9997884
## actor         4.913214e+01    185277.2  2.651818e-04 0.9997884
## beauti        4.913214e+01    185277.2  2.651818e-04 0.9997884
## broke        -1.100742e-14    185277.1 -5.941059e-20 1.0000000
## complet       5.125502e-14    185277.1  2.766398e-19 1.0000000
## custom        4.913214e+01    185277.2  2.651818e-04 0.9997884
## disappoint   -1.004389e-14    185277.1 -5.421011e-20 1.0000000
```

Step 8: Predict on test data

Using the trained model, we predict the probability that each test text is positive. We then convert these probabilities into class labels: if the probability is greater than 0.5, the prediction is "positive", otherwise "negative".

R Code

```
probabilities <- predict(model, test_data,
                      type = "response")
predictions <- ifelse(probabilities > 0.5,
                    "positive", "negative")
```

Step 9: Show predictions vs actual

We create a results data frame that compares the predicted sentiment labels with the actual labels from the test data. Printing this shows where the model performed correctly or made errors.

```
R Code
results <- data.frame(Predicted = predictions,
                      Actual = test_labels)
print(results)
```

```
Output
##    Predicted    Actual
## 3  negative  positive
## 7  negative  negative
```

The results show how well the logistic regression model classified the test samples. For instance, if the model predicted "negative" when the actual label was "positive," that indicates a misclassification. Correct matches indicate the model's ability to learn from the training data.

Wrap-Up

In this lab, we learned how logistic regression can help classify text by turning words into numbers and training a model to predict if a text is positive or negative. Logistic regression gives us easy-to-understand probabilities that show how likely a text belongs to each category. While we worked with a small dataset to keep things simple, the same steps can be applied to much larger sets of data. To get better results, you can try using more data, cleaning the text better, using different ways to weigh words like TF-IDF, or adjusting the model settings. Because it's simple and works well, logistic regression is a good starting point for many text classification problems.

Exercises

Logistic Regression for Text Classification

This lab will practice building logistic regression text classifiers.

Dataset 1: Customer Feedback on Online Shopping

```
R Code
texts1 <- c(
  "The website was easy to navigate,checkout was smooth.",
  "Delivery was late and the package was damaged.",
  "I found exactly what I needed at a great price.",
  "Customer service did not respond to my emails.",
  "Fast shipping and excellent product quality.",
  "Received the wrong item, very frustrating experience.",
  "Great selection and helpful product descriptions.",
  "The return process was complicated and slow.",
  "Very satisfied with my purchase, will buy again.",
  "The product stopped working after a week."
)

labels1 <- c(
  "positive", "negative", "positive",
  "negative", "positive",  "negative",
  "positive", "negative", "positive",
  "negative"
)
```

1. Clean the texts in `texts1` by making everything lowercase, removing punctuation, numbers, common stopwords, and applying stemming.

Then, show the first three cleaned documents.

2. From the cleaned texts, create a Document-Term Matrix (DTM) and display the first four rows and six columns.

3. Convert the DTM into a data frame, add the `labels1` as a factor column named `label`, and show the first six rows.

4. Using `set.seed(42)`, split the data so that 80% is for training and 20% for testing. Show how many positive and negative labels are in each set.

5. Train a logistic regression model using the training data to predict the `label` based on all the word features. Show a summary of the model coefficients.

Dataset 2: Restaurant Reviews

R Code

```
texts2 <- c(
  "The food was excellent and flavorful.",
  "I hated the wait time and rude staff.",
  "Best dining experience I've had this year.",
  "The dessert was too sweet and sickly.",
  "Amazing atmosphere and great service.",
  "Not worth the price, very disappointing.",
  "I would definitely come back here again.",
  "Poor quality and bland dishes.",
  "Staff was attentive and friendly.",
  "The restaurant was dirty and noisy."
)

labels2 <- c(
  "positive", "negative", "positive", "negative", "positive",
  "negative", "positive", "negative", "positive", "negative"
)
```

6. Clean the `texts2` dataset just like before and show the first three cleaned documents.

7. Make a Document-Term Matrix (DTM) from the cleaned text, convert it to a data frame, and add `labels2` as a `label` column. Show the size (rows and columns) of the DTM.

8. Use the first eight rows to train a logistic regression model, then test it on the last two rows. Show the predicted labels alongside the actual labels for the test data.

9. Calculate and report how accurate the model's predictions are on the test set.

www.ingramcontent.com/pod-product-compliance
Lightning Source LLC
Chambersburg PA
CBHW051842210326
41597CB00033B/5745